# LOS ANGELES WINE

# LOS ANGELES WINE

## A History from the Mission Era to the Present

Stuart Douglass Byles

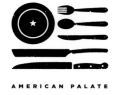

AMERICAN PALATE

Published by American Palate
A Division of The History Press
Charleston, SC 29403
www.historypress.net

Copyright © 2014 by Stuart Douglass Byles
All rights reserved

*Front cover, top*: Vineyard workers in the Lamanda Park (east Pasadena) vineyard of the Sierra Madre Vineyard Co., circa 1890. Hastings Ranch and Echo Mountain are visible in the background. *Courtesy of the archives at Pasadena Museum of History.*

Unless otherwise noted, color images appear courtesy of the author.

First published 2014

Manufactured in the United States

ISBN 978.1.60949.645.6

Library of Congress Control Number: 2014953159

*Notice*: The information in this book is true and complete to the best of our knowledge. It is offered without guarantee on the part of the author or The History Press. The author and The History Press disclaim all liability in connection with the use of this book.

All rights reserved. No part of this book may be reproduced or transmitted in any form whatsoever without prior written permission from the publisher except in the case of brief quotations embodied in critical articles and reviews.

# CONTENTS

Acknowledgements     7
Introduction     11

1. The Spanish Missions: Antecedents     15
2. Early Winemakers and Vineyards     23
3. Jean Louis Vignes, William Wolfskill and the Sainsevains     33
4. The Gold Rush and After     41
5. Developments in the Valleys     49
6. Anaheim: Episode on the Santa Ana     71
7. Rise of the North     75
8. Decline in the South     81
9. Turn of the Century through Prohibition     91
10. From Repeal to the Present     107

Appendix 1. Where Was the Original "Casa" and Vineyard of Jose Maria Verdugo?     121
Appendix 2. Map of the Rancho San Raphael ("La Zanja") and Present-Day Glendale     129
Appendix 3. The Grapes and Wine of Los Angeles, by Mathew Keller     131
Appendix 4. Mathew Keller Obituary     137
Appendix 5. Interview with Georges Le Mesnager     141

## Contents

Appendix 6. Rambaud's Row: Threatens the Life of His Landlord
    and Is Put Under Bonds     143
Bibliography     145
Index     151
About the Author     153

# ACKNOWLEDGEMENTS

No writer writes alone, despite it being a solitary craft. The spirit of those who have helped him, who have gone before and are embodied in memoirs, histories, documents and genealogies all ride on the writer's shoulders, whispering in his ear as he spins his narrative. To those people—known and unknown, met and unmet, past and present—I am deeply grateful for your assistance and counsel. Thank you to the following:

Mike Lawler, my friend and cohort at the Historical Society of the Crescenta Valley, without whose suggestion and encouragement this book would not have been written. Without his continued guidance and help, it also would not have been finished.

Jerry Roberts, my editor, for his solicitude and patience…and patience…and patience.

Thomas Pinney, for his monumental history of wine, which awakened my interest and passion.

Tom and Frances Yeseta, for their innate generosity and unassuming way of winemaking.

Heather D'Agostine, whose gracious, tireless, good-humored mentoring put all of us at the Stonebarn Vineyard Conservancy on the right road of proper viniculture ("Winemaking should be fun!")

The membership of the Stonebarn Vineyard Conservancy, especially Liz and Fred Nelson, Jo Anne and Bill Sadler, Dianne Thompson and Wayne Gilbert, Bruce and Jane Campbell, Sara Stammer, Anne McNeill, Curt and Joan Cleven, Ben and Bambi Fitzsimmons.

## Acknowledgements

The membership of the Historical Society of the Crescenta Valley, especially Pam Lawler, Art Cobery ("just write, and enjoy it as you do!"), Jo Anne Sadler for her manifest suggestions and dedication to the truth, Danette Eriksson, Ellie Pipes, Mike Morgan, Sharon Weisman, John Newcombe and Robert Newcombe.

Bill Weisman, for his time and technical generosity.

Randy Adams, a friend with sage advice, who patiently acted as my sounding board ("Stuart, you should be a university professor!").

Peter Williamson, proofreader extraordinaire, commentator and friend.

John Drayman, for his witty knowledge of the local history and characters.

Cellarmasters, for its continuing work in winemaking, especially members Michael Holland and Dave Lustig.

Cal Poly Pomona Library Special Collections and Archives, for its spectacular wine history collection, and especially Danette Cook Adamson, librarian, for her gracious generosity.

At the Los Angeles Public Library–Special Collections Room at Central: Glen Creason, for his casually serendipitous discovery of the Vignes property survey, and Terri Garst.

John Cahoon at the Los Angeles County Natural History Museum/Seaver Center for Western History.

Matt McLaughlin at the Pasadena Public Library for his efforts in shedding light on Hastings Ranch and Sierra Madre Vintage Co.

Pasadena Museum of History.

Huntington Library.

Patti D'Alessandro from the Sunny Slope Water District, for her kindness and gift of books.

Glendale Public Library Special Collections librarian George Ellison.

Karen and Brian at the La Crescenta County Public Library.

Stephano "Steve" Riboli of the San Antonio Winery, Los Angeles, for his kind generosity, historical detail, his sparkling personality and his recipe for "vinetta."

Don Galleano of the Galleano Winery in Mira Loma, for his generosity and straightforward description of some of the colorful characters in the Southern California wine history.

Gino Filippi of J. Filippi Winery, for his knowledge, as well as generous use of his photo and written archive.

All the local Los Angeles winemakers and vineyard owners who have contributed pictures of their operations and are continuing in this century the great tradition of wine in Los Angeles, especially Jessica and Gary Peterson, John Freeman, Bill Jones, Tim McDonald and the Lustig family.

## Acknowledgements

Los Angeles County Arboretum Gift Shop and Reading Room.
Santa Anita Racetrack.
Alhambra Historical Society, especially Ruth and Eunice for their tireless help, and their friend at Alhambra Camera, David Oswald.
Burbank Historical Society for its insights on the Brusso, Grangetto and McClure wineries.
Blake Gumprecht for his groundbreaking (or should it be river-breaking?) book, *The Los Angeles River*, and permission to use his drawings.

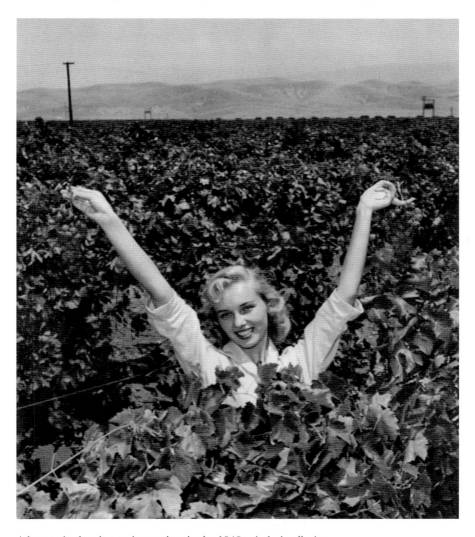

A beauty in the vineyard sometime in the 1940s. *Author's collection.*

## Acknowledgements

Torrey Byles for his inspiring literary example, and Christopher Byles for his "champagne" hosting and history.

City of Glendale council-members for their tacit support of the vineyard; Parks Department head Jesse Duran; and employees Marc Stirdivant, Bill McKinley, Miguel Guzman and Jeff Weinstein for their continuing advice and support; and especially John Pearson, Wilderness Park project manager and visionary, who made the initial overture to the historical society to provide programs on wine history and maintain the vineyard at the Park. It's all your fault, John.

Marie Yeseta, my long-suffering wife, for her patient understanding and support. Maybe she'll have her husband back now.

Any mistakes in the narrative are mine alone. *Mea culpa, mea culpa.*

# INTRODUCTION

*To destroy the relics of the past is, even in small things, a kind of amputation, a self-mutilation not so much of limbs, as of the memory and the imagination.*
—*historian Donald Cameron Watt in* How War Came

Standing on the First Street Bridge just east of Vignes Street looking north, it's hard to imagine this spot as it was for most of the nineteenth century. This area of old downtown Los Angeles (east of Alameda Street) is now a warren of industrial buildings, high-tension wires, freeways, railroad tracks, storage lots and a massive swath of concrete known as the Los Angeles River. Then, it was a greensward: acres of vineyards and vegetable plots, separated by willow-branched, fenced lanes and a winding, willow-shaded river off to the east. On the other side of the river, Boyle Heights was equally green with vineyards and vegetation until it tapered off into the dust of the wide, tree-less plains east and south. Just off to the west was the small town of Los Angeles, a huddle of flat-roofed adobes surrounding its plaza, baking in the brilliant sun of the cloudless, blue skies of Southern California. The only tree in town of any size was the massive, ancient sycamore that grew in the yard of the winery of Jean Louis Vignes and gave the name to his vineyards: El Aliso. From this pioneering French immigrant (who arrived in 1831) came the wine business of California that has grown (like his sycamore) into a huge, statewide industry, making California a force in the world second to none for its quality of wine and technical innovation.

# Introduction

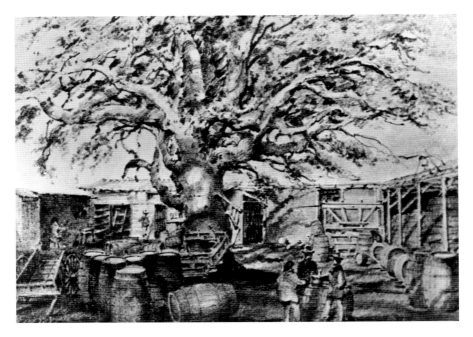

Drawing of Jean Louis Vignes's winery (supposedly in 1831) with his giant sycamore towering over the winery buildings, giving the name to his vineyard operation: El Aliso. *Courtesy of Los Angeles Public Library Photo Collection.*

From its start in Los Angeles, winemaking moved out into the surrounding valleys, planting anew and taking up the old, abandoned vineyards of the San Gabriel and San Fernando missions, out onto the Rancho Cucamonga and down into the Santa Ana River basin. But the "center of gravity" of wineries and their business tended to stay in Los Angeles. As historian Thomas Pinney has written, "For most of the 19th century, California wine meant Los Angeles wine." Only during the great land boom in Southern California of the late 1880s did the vineyards of the center city give way to urbanization; elsewhere, a mysterious vine disease began decimating the vineyards. By that time, northern California began to outpace the south in acres of vines—and varieties—planted. Wineries did remain in Los Angeles, but the grapes came from the valleys. Prohibition closed most of these wineries, until now only one remains in the historic heart of Los Angeles and in its old vineyard area.

All that is left are the street names to commemorate this early history: Vignes, for the man, and Aliso, for his tree and winery; Keller and Mateo Streets for the Irish immigrant winemaker Mathew "Don Mateo" Keller;

# Introduction

Wilson for "Don Benito," the early American mountain man, ranchero, winemaker and Los Angeles mayor; Hoover on the west side of downtown for an early German vineyardist; Mesnager and Bauchet for more French immigrant vignerons; Kohler for the German immigrant musician turned winemaker; and Sainsevain Street for the brothers who inherited their Uncle Vignes's winery, though this inexplicably became Commercial Street after 1884. Ironically, there is a Willow Street by the concrete river, as if in memory of the native trees that used to line the riverbanks.

The gold rush changed the center of population in the state, pushing it radically to the San Francisco Bay area, where it stayed for the next fifty or sixty years. All the world seemed to rush into this place for the opportunities it presented. New immigrants began planting new vineyards, at first with cuttings from the mission stock of vines (San Jose and Sonoma, some even from San Gabriel). It didn't take long before the Santa Clara Valley and then Sonoma, Napa and Livermore valleys were filling up with vineyards and wineries. Sensible men planted vineyards in the Sierra foothills, adjacent to the gold diggings.

There were many other pioneering winemakers in the state, whose energetic, booming voices tended to obscure the fact that the wine trade in California began in the dusty little pueblo beside the Rio Porciuncula.

*Chapter 1*

# THE SPANISH MISSIONS

## *Antecedents*

In 1767, King Charles III of Spain expelled the Jesuits from his court, his kingdom and his empire. This formidable religious order had become over-mighty in its accumulation of power and influence—so much so that the king, quite naturally, feared for his own. The extensive Jesuit mission system in the Spanish new world was divided between the Dominican and Franciscan religious orders. Those missions in Baja California fell to the Franciscans. With them came the directive to establish new missions in the unknown and unexplored areas of Alta California. It was part of the reinvigorated, Spanish imperial spirit, newly revived after more than a century of defeat and disasters. Missions were part of the three-pronged bulwark (mission, presidio and pueblo) with which the Spanish intended to reestablish and protect their centuries-old claim to the Pacific coast of North America from intrusions by other European powers. The military/religious expedition under the command of Gaspar de Portolà and Junipero Serra that set out from Loreto, Baja California, in early 1769 was to do just that.

Slowly, the company made its way up the long, desert peninsula, visiting the established Jesuit missions now under Franciscan control and seeing how primitive the conditions were in this harsh and inhospitable land. Amazingly, the previous owners had been able to establish small vineyards at some of the missions, where arable soil and sufficient rainfall were in very short supply; even vineyards and winemaking containers cut into the solid rock, as historian H. Legett attests.

Resupplied, the members of the party pushed on to their first planned stop in Alta California, the port of San Diego. Their guide was the published account of the voyage of Sebastian Vizcaino in 1602, in which he described the significant ports of San Diego and Monterey. Monterey was the ultimate goal of the enterprise, a port Vizcaino described as one of the finest on the coast, "protected from all winds." It is a description that is—in actuality—entirely false and puzzled the expedition to no end. Reaching the bay of San Diego in July, Serra founded the first mission on the sixteenth, while the military party pushed on to Monterey.

The next several months were a story of starvation, desperation and disaster nearly averted. Had a supply ship not arrived on the afternoon of the date intended for abandonment of the colony, the expedition would have returned down the peninsula in failure. It could have been years before another expedition would have been sent out. Given the close run that was the first mission founding and the known inventories of wine for the Catholic Mass that the expedition carried, it seems implausible that grape cuttings for vineyard planting were part of their provisions. It is a story that started in the late nineteenth century as part of the legend and romance of the missions, that Father Serra planted the first mission grapes at San Diego in 1769. It is a story that is still retold, part of that nostalgic dream of mission days, but it is largely unsupported.

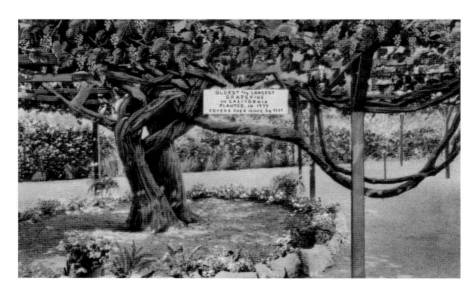

View of the so-called mother grapevine at the San Gabriel mission on an old, hand-tinted postcard from the early 1900s. At that time, the nostalgic legend of the missions and Father Serra was paramount, and the reality was largely unknown. See the narrative related by L.J. Rose Jr. in the surrounding text. *Author's collection.*

A History from the Mission Era to the Present

## First Vines and Vintage

When did the first vines arrive, and where were they planted? Serra constantly complained in his diaries and letters of a lack of wine for the Mass. Barrels of wine were part of the regular mission supply shipments that yearly came out of the port of San Blas on the Mexican mainland, set up for that purpose. But the supply line was long and the missions so remote; the ships' erratic arrivals meant constant privation for the missionaries…and little or no wine. In a letter on October 29, 1783, Serra writes that he had to go to the government stores to buy wine, with no priestly discount! But his next reference to wine is mysteriously cryptic. In a letter of June 18, 1784, all he says is: "But God has provided a way out, and now they [the missions] are well looked after in that respect," as pointed out by historian Roy Brady. What did Serra mean by that? Did the missions actually have producing vineyards? Which ones? Or were they just well stocked with barrels of shipped-in wine? There were only nine missions at that date, four in Southern California, with Ventura only two years old.

By 1777, Serra began sending requests to the governor for vine cuttings to be sent up from Baja California in the next supply ship. He had remembered the vines (and figs and pomegranates that he also requested) growing in the old Jesuit missions there. So vine cuttings were sent by ship, probably the *San Antonio*, under the command of Don Jose Camacho, which arrived in San Diego on May 16, 1778. From where the cuttings came is not certain; they could have been brought to San Blas from inland Mexico, or the ship could have loaded them at a peninsula stopping port; this is a point made by H. Legett. According to Father Francisco Palau's biography of Serra, the decision was made to plant those first cuttings at the San Juan Capistrano mission because of the large amount of wild, native grapevines growing in its valley (vitus sylvestris? girdiana? californicus?). A letter from the priest at San Juan to Father Serra on March 15, 1779, gives the evidence: "Snow is plentiful, wherefore, until the severe cold moderates and the floods subside, the vine cuttings have been buried."

When was the first California vintage? Roy Brady—the noted twentieth-century wine historian already referenced, and the prime source for this portion of the narrative—comes to the conclusion that it was the harvest of 1782 from those vines at San Juan. In a letter written from San Gabriel (somewhat ironic considering the future agricultural empire of that mission) on October 27, 1783, Serra wrote:

> *Many Masses have not been said because of our lack of wine. We have plenty everywhere at present, except at this mission. We met with an accident—when the barrel was being brought here from San Juan Capistrano it fell off the mule, broke into pieces, and all the wine was lost. But the neighboring missions came to the rescue, and will supply the needs in the future.*

Since it became the custom at most missions to harvest as late as possible, often well into October, and the cool beach climate of San Juan Capistrano would also have made a late harvest, that broken barrel would not have contained the 1783 vintage but the previous year's. This is the conclusion of Roy Brady.

## Mission Grape

From these first few cuttings at San Juan Capistrano, the vines were soon taken to all the missions in turn as they were founded. Regardless of its origin in Mexico (or Baja)—its genetic heritage is still uncertain—the grape shares biological and ampelographic characteristics with an old Spanish variety called Monica or Criolla. Widely planted in South America, it thrives to this day in Argentina, Peru and especially in Chile, where it is second only to cabernet sauvignon in acreage. The Spanish brought it to their mission settlements in the Rio Grande river valley of the seventeenth century, in what are now Texas and New Mexico. In California, its close association with the missions gave the grape its name, and for over a century, it dominated winemaking in the state. The characteristics of the vine—strength, disease resistance and high productivity—ensured that dominance until the prominence of European immigrant winemakers and changing tastes in the late nineteenth century caused its fall from favor. For the padres—with their Spanish/Mediterranean heritage—the Mission grape was a perfect choice and found a natural home in the hills and valleys of California, especially the warmer southern half.

A History from the Mission Era to the Present

## Spread of Viticulture

Vineyard growing at each of the missions met with varying success. At the San Francisco mission—Dolores—there was no vineyard at all because of the cold and wet climate. But the padres did have a winery to make wine from grapes grown at San Jose and Santa Clara. Santa Cruz was not successful at growing vines, and neither was Carmel, sharing that cold and foggy climate. San Raphael and Santa Clara were successful, but the largest of the northern missions was San Jose, with some estimates of over eleven thousand vines (difficult to estimate precisely on all mission properties). The smallest was the Sonoma mission, where a British traveler visiting General Vallejo in the 1840s estimated it at approximately three hundred square feet. All down the chain were varying sizes at each of the missions. Some estimates of San Luis Obispo's vineyard put it at forty acres, second only to San Gabriel. San Buenaventura's was equal to San Jose. San Luis Rey had a large establishment; so did San Diego, probably planted in the same or next season as those first vine cuttings at San Juan Capistrano (1779–80). San Fernando had the second-largest vineyard (planted in two adobe-walled gardens) of approximately thirty-two thousand vines at its height.

But all paled in comparison to the vineyards of San Gabriel. Some estimates put it at over 163,000 vines, some at 146,000. Estimating mission viticulture is difficult because of conflicting numbers at the secularization of the missions by the Mexican government in 1833. At whatever amount, the large-scale winemaking operation was commensurate (at its height) with the mission's overall vast agricultural empire that stretched over the San Gabriel valley and on into the Pomona valley to its *assistencia* at San Bernardino. Over the sixty-five-mile length of the two valleys, the padres ran cattle and sheep and planted wheat, olives and oranges, all the while tending to the spiritual health and conversion of the natives, their main focus.

Much of this expansion—agricultural and physical—came from the energies of José Zalvidea during his long tenure (1806–27) as mission father. It was he who brought the mission to its dominant place in the amount of vines under cultivation, winery capacity and quality (at least to some) of its wines and brandies. Much has been written about the "Mother Vineyard" there, usually misconstruing it to be the mother of all the mission vineyards. It was only the "mother" of the several large vineyards that Zalvidea planted over the huge mission property in the San Gabriel Valley. As of this writing, Michael Hart, a local artist and retired *zanjero* of the Sunny Slope Water District, has done long research into the mission and water history of

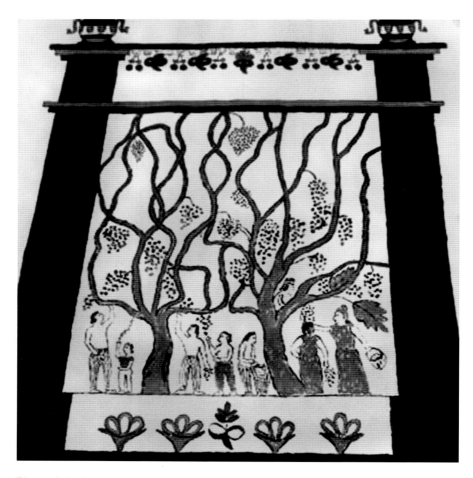

Photo of the fresco painting at San Fernando mission showing Indians harvesting grapes. It is interesting to surmise from the picture that the missionaries planted the vines to grow into neighboring trees as a means of support. This is an ancient method from Italy and Spain. *Author's photo, but courtesy of the San Fernando mission.*

the area. His results are in a unique "painted map" showing at least five separate vineyards, with some close to the mission and others strewn along the Raymond escarpment streams and canyons just to the north.

With the missions being so remote from the centers of empire, the padres had no choice but to rely on clever use of materials at hand. Winemaking was no different. With their cattle herds abundant, cowhides sealed with the local tar (such as from the La Brea pits) were used to form large wineskins. Pig hides made the smaller *bota* bags. These were a staple of Spanish winemaking in the old country. Wooden barrels made the long sea voyage from the mainland. As the mission system became more developed, the padres began making their own barrels from the local forests; the California tradition of using redwood wine barrels may date from this time. Vineyards were laid out in lines of single-vine "bushes," grown on a support stake and then "head-pruned." This method continued long into the later periods and is sometimes still seen today. The ubiquitous wire treillage on posts in today's vineyards was a French invention of the later nineteenth century. Often part of the crushing and fermentation took place in a large outdoor vat, made of plastered-over adobe. Crude and rudimentary, to say the least, was the norm. Yet mission winemaking was the genesis of all future California winemaking.

## Mexican Independence and Secularization

Just as the missions were reaching the apogee of their development, Mexico (and the two Californias) declared its independence from Spain in 1821. Suddenly all the Spanish and Indian populations were Mexican citizens. Not much changed. The settlements in Alta California were so far removed from the centers of control and easy interchange, so remote on the far edge of the world, that they might as well have been colonies on the moon.

Yet one thing did change. The Mexican government encouraged foreign exchange, whereas the Spanish government jealously kept out all other influence, except that of the home country. As a result, ships from other countries began finding their way to the coast and ports of California. Parched from long sea voyages, the captains and crews welcomed the wines the missions had to offer. The various surviving letters, ships' logs and diaries from that time reflect the discernment, comparison and hearsay evidence about the mission product that was tasted. A French sea captain, Auguste Bernard Duhaut-Cilly, in his 'round-the-world voyage, visited the San Luis Rey mission in June 1827 and left an admiring account of the grand building program and its vineyard, writing, "These orchards grow the most exquisite olives and produce the best grapewine in all California. I took a sample of this wine with me and I have it still. I kept it seven years. It has the taste of the Paxaret and the color of the *porto purgato*."

According to Thomas Pinney, paxaret is similar to the sweet, liquor-like wine Angelica for which Los Angeles became famous. Duhaut-Cilly also sampled the grapes of Los Angeles and thought they were good, but "the wines and brandies made from them were very inferior…and I think this inferiority is to be attributed to the making rather than the growth." Given the primitive conditions of winemaking at the time, getting an acceptable result that would satisfy a knowledgeable palate such as Duhaut-Cilly's would be somewhat miraculous. On an expedition from the Hudson Bay Company in 1842, Sir Alexander Simpson traveled through California during the Mexican period and took a dim view of the remaining mission wine, calling most of it "utter trash." However, visiting the Santa Barbara mission, he had a favorable change of mind, writing, "Most of the stuff which we had tasted, we should have carried away with out compunction, thinking we were doing the owners a service; but we were sorry to deprive the very reverend donor, in the present state of his cellar, of a really good article."

Father Duran, the head of the San Jose mission and winemaker there, thought that the best wines of the system as a whole came from the San Gabriel mission. A German traveler at San Jose, Langstorff thought the wines there resembled a good Malaga style, a Spanish sweet wine.

The rumblings from Mexico City since independence to dismantle the mission system in favor of the Indian natives finally occurred in 1833. The church was forced to hand over its lands and possessions to civilian authorities for distribution. The clergy members were left only with their spiritual duties as local parish priests. For the developed economy that the missions had accomplished in sixty-four years, it was a disaster. The thriving agriculture was let go—in some cases, willfully destroyed—by the grief-stricken priests in protest. With it went the natives, who—bewildered by the events—began disappearing from the only home they had known. In only a few years, what had taken so long to build was in ruins. Now the pace of "land grant" ranchos picked up, as local Spanish/Mexican families and newly arrived immigrants staked claims on the former mission properties. Some of the agriculture was kept up or kept up in severely reduced circumstances. Most was let go or taken off the land to other properties.

Despite the despoliation of the missions themselves, for vineyards and winemaking, it was a seamless transition from church lands to civilian hands; its evolution continued unabated on into the American period. For the future of California winemaking, it was serendipitous that it was Spain (and its mission system) that colonized the Pacific coastline. It brought its Mediterranean wine heritage to a new Mediterranean-style climate; it brought a vinifera grape to be grown for its use in the religious services and an attitude that wine was a beverage enjoyed (and necessary) as a daily part of life.

*Chapter 2*

# EARLY WINEMAKERS AND VINEYARDS

Part of the Spanish "trinity" of colonization (mission, presidio and pueblo) consisted of founding towns, a civilian component to complement the military and theological authorities. The first Alta California pueblo was founded at San Jose on the Guadalupe River in 1777, near the south end of San Francisco Bay. The second was to be somewhere in the southern area. Portola's expedition had passed by an Indian settlement called Yangna next to a large river (by Southern California standards) as it debouched from a narrows formed by a series of hills and mountains. An expansive plain southeast and west would provide for agricultural expansion. The site seemed to bode well for a town. The expedition noted that wild grapevines and roses abounded next to willow trees along the riverbanks. A stately sycamore tree stood on the west side of the river, providing a shady gathering spot on the otherwise treeless plain. In September 1781, the first settlers of the new pueblo of Nuestra Senora de la Reina de Los Angeles de Porciuncula made the nine-mile trek from the San Gabriel mission to found the town.

The name of whoever was the first to plant a vineyard in the new pueblo along the Rio Porciuncula is lost to history, but it must have been one of those first settlers. Obviously, they obtained cuttings from the mission, but this was much later after the vineyards had been established. The native grapevines growing in abundance turned out to be useless for winemaking to the Spanish taste. However, the first civilian vineyard in the Los Angeles area as well as Alta California appears to be that of José Maria Verdugo. He was one of three soldiers of the guard at the San Gabriel mission who received

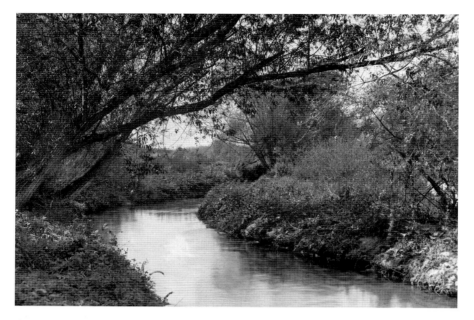

Los Angeles River near downtown around 1900. The river's natural, willow-lined trace is still extant at this date, showing the attractions that moved the Spanish to found the pueblo in this area. The constantly running river, and the *zanjas* leading from it, was the key ingredient for the success of vineyards, agriculture and the town. *Courtesy of the Seaver Center for Western History, Natural History Museum of Los Angeles.*

cattle-grazing permits from the governor in October 1784. Over time, these permits turned into permanent grants of land, making those old soldiers the first rancheros. Verdugo's Rancho San Rafael lay just outside the pueblo limits, starting at a point where the Arroyo Hondo (now Arroyo Seco) meets the Rio Porciuncula (Los Angeles River) and fans out to the north. Most of today's cities of Glendale and Burbank, with portions of Pasadena and Los Angeles, are in its boundaries.

Just where his vineyard was and when he planted it is not yet known. But there is some circumstantial evidence to suggest a general area and timeline. Jose Maria Verdugo rarely called his rancho by its legal title but usually called it more affectionately "La Zanja" (the water ditch or weir). In 1795, missionaries began looking for a new mission site. Their diaries mentioned that they stopped at the "paraje de la zanja" (the place of the water ditch) just below Cahuenga Peak, where they spoke to some of Verdugo's workers and noted his vegetable garden. Very likely he could have had a vineyard at that time. That would put the zanja at the west side of his rancho, right at the great curve of the Rio

# A History from the Mission Era to the Present

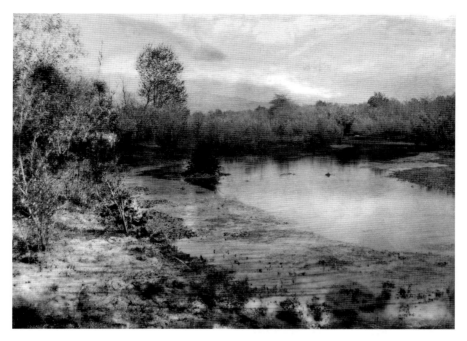

Los Angeles River near Griffith Park around 1900. Because of the particular geology of the Narrows and its outflow near the pueblo, the river was a year-round stream along this section. This was not so in its sources in the San Fernando Valley, nor miles south of town. In storm times, this shallow trace became a wide flood, destroying much of the riverside vineyards. *Courtesy of the Seaver Center for Western History, Natural History Museum of Los Angeles.*

where it turns south and enters (what came to be known then and now as) the Narrows, just above the entrance of Verdugo Creek. Considering that future vineyards were in this area all throughout the nineteenth century and into the twentieth, it would make sense that he would have established his operation (and his home) in this area, close to (but out of the way of) surging river water. By that 1795 date, he was well on his way to patenting his rancho, which he finally did in 1798, the same year as those inquiring padres established the San Fernando mission. Because of his duties at the San Gabriel mission, he had every opportunity to get his grape cuttings from there once the vineyards there had been well established. That "paraje de la zanja" is currently the site of the ABC television studios in Glendale.

Antonio Lugo, who planted vines not long after 1809 in the pueblo itself, is the first vinyardist known by name, according to Thomas Pinney. Later, he built a two-story residence (the only one for a time) facing the plaza. More land down along the river was planted in vines, so that by 1818, an estimated fifty-three thousand vines had been put in. Families like the Vejar, Tapia, Requena and Yorba all had vineyards in the area most likely from this early date.

The first known American to plant a vineyard was Joseph Chapman in 1826. His colorful entrance into Southern California history was as a pirate, crewing with the buccaneer Hippolyte Bouchard. Though born in France, Bouchard flew the Argentinian flag as he made a 'round-the-world voyage in 1817–19 to plunder all things Spanish. Stopping in Hawaii, he shanghaied several new crew members, one of them Chapman. Born in Boston, Massachusetts, Chapman was a polymath and sailor who found his world changed again when he was captured by the Spanish when Bouchard raided the California coast in 1818. Brought to Los Angeles under "house arrest" by Antonio Lugo, he soon showed his principled ways and was freed. A natural engineer and builder, he became indispensible to the padres at San Gabriel. He built a grain mill just south of the mission when the older one in Mill Canyon proved faulty. He surveyed and oversaw the building of a water retention dam (La Presa) to run the mill on a creek to the north. It was still in use when L.J. Rose acquired the land for his vineyards in the 1860s. Today, it is still extant on the property of the Sunny Slope Water District. Chapman, known as "Jose Huero"—Joe White or Blonde Joe—to his Spanish friends, put in approximately four thousand vines down by the river near the pueblo, not far from the Plaza church that he built in the early 1820s. His son still ran the vineyard long after his father retired to end his days in Santa Barbara, the very place where he had been captured in his pirate days with Bouchard.

At almost the same time as Chapman was planting his vineyard, Louis Bauchet arrived in the pueblo in 1827. He had been a soldier in Napoleon's Imperial Guard and was the first of that French immigration to Los Angeles that played such an important part in the life of the town over the next decades. He bought land, planted a vineyard and prospered until his death in 1852. He was a neighbor and friend of Victor Prudhomme and Jean Louis Vignes, his countrymen; Vignes arrived in 1831.

Farther down Alameda Street were the vineyards of William Wolfskill, an American who arrived in 1833, and the Swiss immigrant Leonce Hoover (his name changed from the German "Huber").

Another neighbor and friend of Bauchet and Vignes was Juan M. Ramirez, who arrived from Santa Barbara in 1828 and established a vineyard that later was taken over by his son, Juan Reincarnacion Ramirez. Their vineyard was near the current Los Angeles city archives building, Denny's restaurant and where the 101 Freeway crosses the street that is named after them. Juan's older brother, Francisco, published the first Spanish-language newspaper in town, *El Clamor Publico*, which ran from 1855 to 1859. He was a close friend of his neighbor Jean Louis Vignes and would spend hours discussing local politics and events. Their sister Isabel, too, was in the wine business, as she married the Italian wine merchant Antonio Pelanconi, whose winery building on Wine Street (now Olvera Street) still stands as of this date; it now houses the La Golondrina restaurant. With her second husband, Giacomo Tononi (her first husband's associate), she reacquired a large portion of her family's vineyard in the 1880s.

Still another European, this time from the Netherlands, arrived in 1828 and started his own vineyard. Johann van Groningen had been shipwrecked on the coast of San Pedro Bay, supposedly on a Sunday, and his soon-to-be Spanish friends gave him the name of Juan Domingo. He was a carpenter by trade and later added a winery to his vineyard business.

Across the river on the slopes rising up to the eastside heights, Jose Rubio planted a vineyard and named it after the bluffs that over looked it: Paredon Blanco. The vineyard continued into the American period, when Andrew Boyle, an Irish immigrant to Los Angeles in the 1850s, bought it from Rubio.

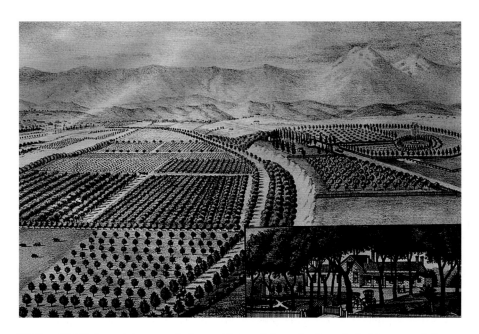

William H. Workman's home and vineyard/citrus "plantation" on the heights east of the Los Angeles River, circa 1860s. His uncle of the same name was a partner with Rowland in a large rancho in La Puente. *Courtesy of the Los Angeles Public Library Photo Collection.*

He expanded its operation, kept the vineyard name, added wine cellars and built a large two-story brick home on the heights that now bear his family name. His son-in-law—William H. Workman—named the area after his wife and again expanded the vineyard while adding orange and other fruit trees. Workman also developed the land into a wealthy suburb, beginning what would be the tried-and-true method of landownership in the Southland and the ultimate downfall of its iconic agriculture of vineyards and citrus groves.

During the Spanish period, the families of mission and presidio soldiers lived in the local pueblos. Only a few grants of land were given out during that time. When the Mexican government began the expropriation of the mission property after 1833, land grants became the norm. The rewarded soldiers and their families began moving out onto their new property, building homes, planting the required *fanegas* of wheat, running cattle and planting vineyards and fruit orchards, or, in the case of Andres Pico, continuing and reviving the vineyards and orchards of the San Fernando mission. Many families still maintained residences in the pueblo, along with their rancho adobes.

Tiburcio Tapia acquired the Rancho Cucamonga—near the San Bernardino assistancia of mission San Gabriel—in 1839, the year he was

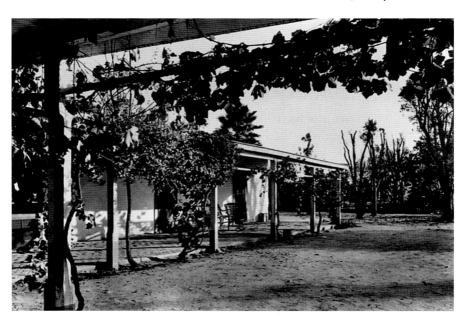

Courtyard and grape trellis of Wolfskill adobe. Photographed at the time of the property's subdivision in the land boom of the 1880s and the subsequent demolition of the adobe. *Courtesy of Los Angeles Public Library Photo Collection.*

## A History from the Mission Era to the Present

*alcalde* (mayor) of the *ayuntamiento* (town council). He moved onto his new 13,100-acre holdings and began planting vineyards near his new adobe in an area called Red Hill (just west of Foothill Boulevard and Vineyard Avenue in Rancho Cucamonga). He had the example of his father, Jose Bartolome Tapia, who had been granted the Rancho Topanga-Malibu-Sequit in 1804 for his military service. Jose was a cattle rancher and is not known to have planted vines. Vineyards on the Malibu came later. His daughter married a French immigrant, Leon Victor Prudhomme, and together they inherited the rancho. Prudhomme also attempted to patent the Rancho Topanga in the American period but was unsuccessful, finally selling his interest to the Irish immigrant winemaker Mathew Keller.

Not too many years later, and not too far from Rancho Cucamonga, a newly arrived American immigrant purchased the Rancho Jurupa (today, the city of Riverside) from its short-termed original owner, Juan Bandini. Benjamin Davis Wilson had arrived in Southern California in 1841 with a group of his trapper associates in the Rowland-Workman party, determined to continue on to China. Born in Tennessee in 1811, he had come out of St. Louis as a trapper at the age of twenty-two, working the southern Rocky Mountains and confronting the dangers of Indian attacks, bears and mortal wounds. At one point, he barely escaped his Indian captors, running naked into the mountains, before they roasted him alive. Ironically, it was native California Indians who saved his life as a grizzly bear almost killed him—twice—not too far from his home on the Rancho Jurupa. Settling into Santa Fe as a storekeeper for a time, he soon moved on to California. According to his records, his attempts to leave for China were unsuccessful, "and receiving so much kindness from the native Californians I arrived at the conclusion that there was no place in the world where I could enjoy more true happiness and true friendship than among them, there were no courts, no juries, no lawyers, nor any need for them. The people were honest and hospitable, and their word was as good as their bond."

Davis bought the rancho in 1843. It allowed him to keep his American citizenship and Protestant faith, as the rancho was far away from the sea. Mexican law forbade foreigners from owning any property close to the ocean, and those foreign immigrants who did had become Mexican citizens, converted to Catholicism and taken local girls as wives.

Wilson did marry the daughter of his neighbor (of many miles away) Don Bernardo Yorba, who owned the 150,000-acre Rancho Santa Ana (present-day Orange County). Yorba lived in an eighty-room, two-story adobe with wraparound verandahs in the form of a Monterey colonial style. In its daily operation, it was a mini-pueblo, with all that entailed to sustain the rancho's main occupation of cattle raising. Yorba, too, raised a quantity of grapes. The youngest of his four children was Ramona, who married Wilson in February 1844. She was fifteen; Wilson was thirty-two. Nine months later,

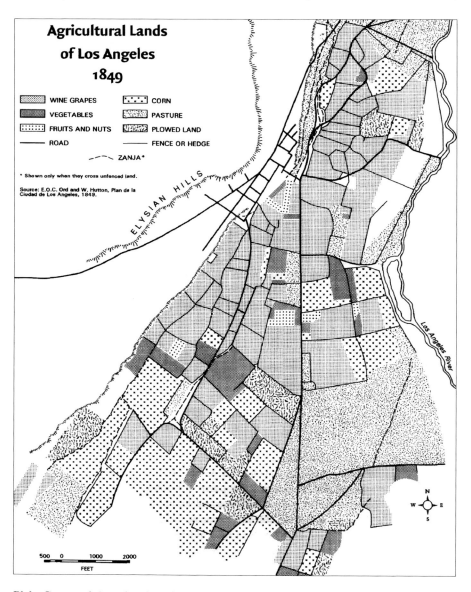

Blake Gumprecht's re-drawing of agricultural lands from Lieutenant Ord's 1849 map/survey of the pueblo of Los Angeles. *Courtesy of Blake Gumprecht*, The Los Angeles River.

their first child was born, a daughter. They named her after Ramona's mother, Maria de Jesus Alvarado, who had died in Ramona's birth. Called Sue by her family, she would be important in the later development of her father's winemaking career. A son, John B., followed in December 1846.

On the Rancho Jurupa, Wilson built an adobe house, complete with a deep cellar for his wine and brandy operation. But his main occupation—like most other rancheros—was running cattle. By 1847, he had a store and a second home in the pueblo of Los Angeles. He disposed of his two thousand head of cattle on a long drive to Sutter's Fort, selling them in the months prior to Marshall's discovery of gold. Back in Los Angeles, he sold his rancho to Louis Robidoux and began planting vines next to his home on Alameda Street near Vine Street (or Wine Street, now Olvera Street) on the edge of town.

The future looked bright for the inhabitants of the little pueblo as the American occupation began. Wilson and his neighbors—Vignes, Wolfskill, Ramirez, Bauchet, Hoover and the rest—lived in a village of green fields, gurgling water ditches (*zanjas*, a major feature of early Los Angeles, with the *zanjero* more important than the mayor) and willow-shaded lanes leading down to the shallow-running river, with over one hundred vineyards in the city and its immediate vicinity. The treaty that ended the Mexican-American War in 1848 guaranteed the Mexican citizens in the newly won American areas secure title to their lands and possessions. The simple, uncomplicated life in the Southland, with a few new settlers, could continue undisturbed—or so it seemed.

However, with the avalanche of immigration that was about to descend on the state, it was not to be.

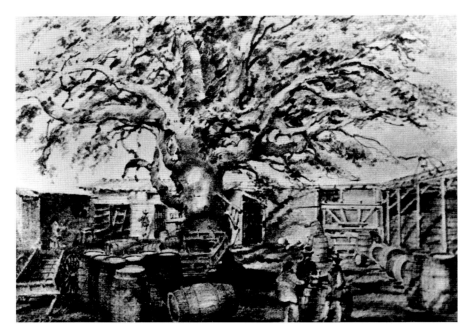

Drawing of Jean Louis Vignes's winery (supposedly in 1831) with his giant sycamore towering over the winery buildings, giving the name to his vineyard operation: El Aliso. *Courtesy of Los Angeles Public Library Photo Collection.*

*Chapter 3*

# JEAN LOUIS VIGNES, WILLIAM WOLFSKILL AND THE SAINSEVAINS

## Jean Louis Vignes (1780–1862)

With the arrival of Jean Louis Vignes in Los Angeles, winemaking underwent a significant change. If a man's name is his destiny, then Vignes ("vines," in French) is so appropriate to the wine trade. In the arc of his career, Vignes showed the way forward in the making and selling of wine. He and his winemaking methods were not well known statewide, but in Los Angeles, he was respected and popular. Because of his pioneering ways and contributions to commercial viticulture, he rightly deserves to be called the "father of winemaking in California."

What would make a forty-six-year-old, middle-aged man—or a man closing in on his dotage for that time period—uproot himself from all he had known, leave his wife and family and travel to the unknown, far side of the world? Yet in 1826, Jean Louis Vignes did just that. Born in a small village near Cadillac on the Gironde River in the Bordeaux wine region of France, his family had been in the wine business for generations. Vignes was a wine cooper by trade. He married, had children and became a respected member of the community. For whatever reason (some say it was because of his generosity to people on the wrong side of politics; others say it was involvement in a particular religious group, and the French priest he traveled with, later became the parish priest in Los Angeles), he left home, boarded a ship headed for South America, sailed around its tip and landed in Hawaii.

He ran a rum distillery until the Hawaiian king—under pressure from a local Puritan minister from New England—put a stop to that. Unable to find more work, he shipped out for California in 1831. On the same ship was his future great friend William Heath Davis, who was not even ten years old at the time. After landing in Monterey, Vignes arrived in Los Angeles at an unknown date. But by 1833, he had a vineyard and one hundred acres of land east of the pueblo, along the river. He built flat-roofed, adobe winery buildings around a magnificent and ancient sycamore tree. The natives called it El Aliso out of respect. It became the symbol and the name of his operation and his own pueblo honorific, Don Luis del Aliso.

As he developed his wine and brandy making, he realized he would have to do better than the Mission grape if he was going to make a better wine. He sent to France for the grape varieties of his Bordeaux homeland. One can only speculate on what they were and how much they were part of his wines. His product always had a high reputation, but—according to Thomas Pinney—no later winemaker (other than his nephews) claimed to have planted Vignes's French imports nor claimed him as a mentor.

With enough aged wine in storage and his nephew Pierre Sainsevain to help him, he arranged for a wine shipment up the coast to the San Francisco Bay, stopping at Santa Barbara and Monterey en route. This first shipping venture in 1840 was only occasionally followed up in the Mexican period, though he had made money on the effort.

With his encouragement, most of his family joined him: three of his five children, with their families; his younger brother; four nephews; and many friends of the family. The expanding "Frenchtown" (as the area came to be known for some time thereafter) and colony was centered around his winery. It is hard to estimate the population of the French expatriate community of the time; some researchers have put it in the range of 400 to 600. In a town of 1,200 to 1,400 souls, it was decidedly influential: for a time, more French was heard on the streets of Los Angeles than English. But Jean Louis never saw his wife, Jeanne, again; she died in 1842 in France.

Don Luis was respected and liked by his neighbors and pueblo natives. He built a quarter-mile-long vine trellis from his winery to the river that was a popular social gathering spot. He was a fairly regular petitioner at the pueblos's *ayuntamiento* (city council), often requesting new land, protesting a fence encroachment and once asking that the river be moved and straightened where it ran by his vineyard. Visiting foreigners wrote favorably about his character and his wines. He even sent a barrel of his creation to the king of France by long sea voyage, but it burned in a warehouse fire in

## A History from the Mission Era to the Present

Hamburg, Germany, while waiting transshipment. Much of what is known about Vignes and his work is by William Heath Davis in his memoir *Seventy-Five Years in California*. He had known the man since childhood and thought he was "one of the most valuable men who ever came to California, and the father of the wine industry here." He was impressed by the age of some of the El Aliso wine; so often, the locals drank theirs right after fermentation. Davis also listened to Vignes describing the future of California winemaking, stating that it could equal or surpass that of France.

Vignes continued to expand his vineyards in the American period, buying land across the river near a new Irish neighbor, Andrew Boyle. He also planted orange groves from stock from the old San Gabriel mission, as did another neighbor to the south, William Wolfskill. By the time of the gold rush in 1849, he had the largest vineyards in the pueblo (which also meant the state), with more than forty thousand vines and producing one thousand barrels of wine a year. He was a patentee of the Rancho Temecula (anticipating that area's possibilities for winemaking).

In 1855, he decided to retire and sold his winery and vineyards to his nephews Pierre and Jean Louis Sainsevain for the then unheard of price of $42,000. He spent the rest of his life doing civic works and enhancing the life of the French "colony," many members of which had come at his urging. He

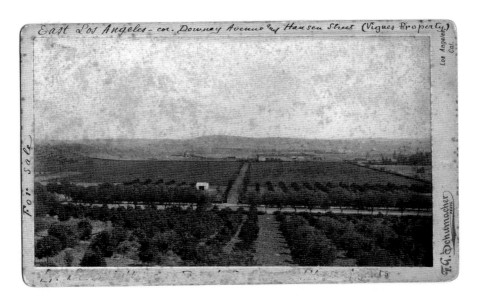

J.L. Vignes's property, showing his vines and citrus orchards in the 1870s, on the east side of the river. *Courtesy of the Seaver Center for Western History, Natural History Museum of Los Angeles.*

is buried in the Evergreen Cemetery of Los Angeles. Let Davis's summation of the life of Don Luis be his epitaph: "It is to be hoped that historians will do justice to his character, his labors and foresight."

## William Wolfskill (1798–1866)

William Wolfskill was born in Kentucky but raised on the frontier of Missouri. He arrived in Taos, New Mexico, with the first American trading mission in 1822. Living and trading in Taos, he traveled to El Paso del Norte to try its "Pass Wine" as an item for trade. The vines and winemaking of the El Paso and Rio Grande areas were of an older Spanish era than even the California missions. There, the Mission grape variety had been planted by Spanish padres in the late seventeenth century. Wolfskill continued trapping and trading across the Southwest until he arrived in Los Angeles in 1833. He bought an existing vineyard from its Mexican owner and continued to add land and vines. He traded for a larger piece of land south of the pueblo, still on Alameda, building an even larger winery and vineyard. He was a steady producer, adding more land and vines, selling to other winemakers and making brandy.

He helped his brother John to obtain a land grant from General Vallejo in what became Solano County and stocked it with vines from his and the

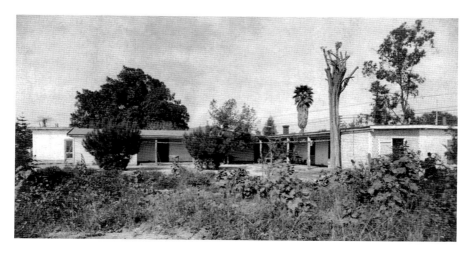

William Wolfskill's residence and winery at the time of subdivision in the 1880s. *Courtesy of Los Angeles Public Library Photo Collection.*

San Gabriel mission vineyards. Wolfskill's wines won awards at the state fair in 1856 and 1859, with some admirers saying it compared with the best of French wines. At the beginning of the 1860s, he was producing fifty thousand gallons a year. In 1865, he bought Hugo Ried's Rancho Santa Anita, expanding its vineyards and wine production. He died the next year, and his sons continued the business.

Wolfskill planted extensive orange orchards (far more than his neighbor Jean Louis Vignes) and developed the methods of their tending—so much so that he is considered the pioneer citrus grower in the state.

## Sainsevain Brothers: Pierre (1818–1904) and Jean Louis (1817–1889)

After Jean Louis Vignes had been gone for over ten years, his eldest nephew, Pierre, set out to find out what had happened to him. In 1839, his long journey finally brought him to Los Angeles, where Pierre began working for the El Aliso Winery. Vignes sent word back to his family and friends that he was fine and that California was the place to live and thrive. As a result, many of his countrymen moved to the little pueblo. It is not known just how many Jean Louis convinced to come out, but his namesake nephew (Pierre's brother) was one of them.

Pierre was the leader of that first wine shipment voyage to San Francisco, as Don Luis was teaching his nephew (soon to be called Don Pedro) all the facets of the wine business. Vignes had established a sawmill near what

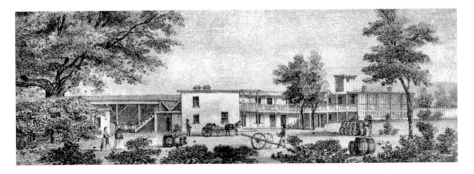

View of Jean Louis Vignes's winery right after he sold it to his nephews, the Sainsevain brothers. From the Kuchel and Dresel illustration of 1857. *Courtesy of Los Angeles Public Library Photo Collection.*

First page of a letter to Pierre Sainsevain from his nephew Vidal Vignes. The letter is postmarked 1845 from Cadillac, France, the Bordeaux-area hometown of the Vignes and Sainsevain families. Vidal later joined his uncles in Los Angeles. *Courtesy of the Seaver Center of Western History, Natural History Museum of Los Angeles.*

# A History from the Mission Era to the Present

would become San Bernardino to have a ready supply of wooden barrels for wine storage. Pierre worked there for a few years before starting another sawmill in 1843 in Santa Cruz, the first in that river valley. In the same year, he was granted by the governor the Rancho Canada del Rincon del Rio San Lorenzo near his sawmill. He began another milling project—this time a flour mill—in San Jose, where he met and married Paula Sunol,

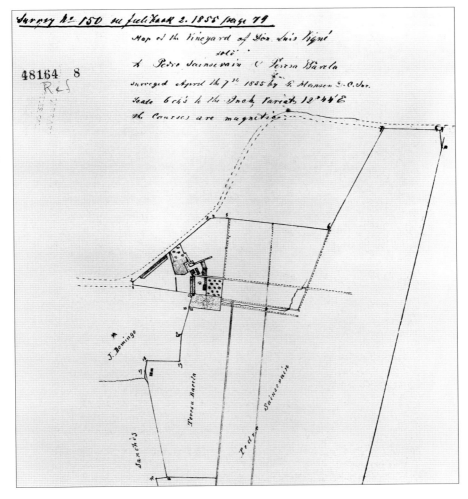

This 1855 survey of J.L. Vignes's property was part of the deed of sale to his nephews, the Sainsevain brothers. The surveyor was George Hansen, the Austrian immigrant who, in the next year, was organizing the Los Angeles Vineyard Society and surveying its new vineyard property on the lower Santa Ana River. It became known as Anaheim. *Author's photo of the map courtesy of the Los Angeles Public Library.*

the daughter of a Spanish ranchero. His varied career and connection with northern California continued with a sailing expedition to Hawaii, gold mining near Coloma and an appointment as a representative to the California Constitutional Convention in Monterey in 1849. He sold his Santa Cruz rancho to return to Los Angeles and join with his brother, Jean Louis, in buying their uncle's winery, El Aliso, in 1855.

The brothers quickly expanded the size and scope of their uncle's operation in preparation for a larger presence in San Francisco to supply wine to gold miners. They bought wine and grapes from other growers and vintners, opening their Bay-area store in 1857. By 1858, they led the state in production with 125,000 gallons of wine and brandy, according to Pinney. They had become entranced with the idea of champagne, and one brother returned to France to learn the steps. He returned with a champagne maker in tow. Their first vintage was 1857–58, which they shipped to New York and Philadelphia. But it was not successful. Mission grapes are not the right variety for champagne, but it was all they had. Much of their loss came from bottle breakage. Their champagne venture was a financial disaster for the brothers and was one factor in the breakup of their partnership in the 1860s. Pierre returned to the San Francisco Bay area, leaving Jean Louis at El Aliso. But Jean Louis sold the old winery in 1865.

The brothers helped John Rains—the new owner of the Rancho Cucamonga—plant 175,000 vines on the property and then set up and managed his winery. After Rains was murdered out on the plains near his rancho, the brothers—abruptly out of work—moved on to other pursuits.

After the death of his wife, Pierre returned to France and died there. Jean Louis stayed in Los Angeles, and in 1862, he received a contract to build a new water system for the city. In 1865, with the help of former mayor and countryman Damien Marchessault, Sainsevain built a water wheel to supply a refurbished flume system. With another contract in late 1867, Jean Louis was to replace wooden pipes with iron, but floods washed away the dam that impounded the water that fed the wheel, and it, too, was washed away. Completely humiliated for his part in the fiasco, Marchessault shot himself in Common Council chambers in January 1868. In the last line of his suicide note, he begs forgiveness from Mr. Sainsevaine for the debt he owes. In his own despair, Jean Louis sold his water lease to another group of investors.

*Chapter 4*

# THE GOLD RUSH AND AFTER

Most estimates of California population at the time of annexation by the United States are just that. But rough figures put the European population at around 13,000–14,000. Even more difficult to arrive at is a population number for the native Indians. Their numbers had been in decline for years, decimated by the diseases carried by succeeding movements of Spanish, Mexican, European and American immigrants who were immune. But by the census of 1852, just four years after the Treaty of Guadalupe-Hidalgo, California had 224,000 residents. The world had literally "rushed in" to become rich mining the gold fields of California.

This incredible immigration and the massive changes that it brought have been well studied by historians. Social and legal institutions in the new state struggled and failed to cope. But a freewheeling economy developed out of the chaos. Those economic opportunities for slaking the thirst of the hordes of miners in the gold fields of the Sierra Nevada were not lost on the winemakers of Los Angeles. Soon enough, they were making regular shipments to the markets of San Francisco and Sacramento. Not only wine and brandy but also fresh grapes went north. As Thomas Pinney succinctly says, "San Francisco was where the wine was drunk, but Los Angeles was where it was made." This defined the relationship of the two sections of the state for decades, until the dominance of Los Angeles winemaking was equaled and then surpassed by the Bay Area wine regions in the latter nineteenth century.

The new arrivals from the East Coast and elsewhere who had experience in winemaking were astounded to see the thriving vineyards of Southern

California. They were quick to see that the mild, dry climate with the fertile soil was almost perfect for viticulture. The centuries-long attempt at transplanting European vines to the American colonies on the East Coast, and then the new republic, had been met by repeated failure. Winemaking in the east was left with using the native labrusca and rupestris grapes, with their natural "foxiness" taste that was not to everyone's satisfaction. Yet here in this new land were fields upon fields of vineyards with wineries making a wine of distinctively European taste, despite the flaws of the Mission grape itself and the unknowing and crude winemaking methods that were used. It wasn't long before California was being touted as the "vineland of the world."

Los Angeles had its share of population growth at this time, and not always for the better. Robbers, con artists, thieves and other morally bankrupt men from the mining areas up north made their way to the southern part of the state to set up their brand of "money-making." The crime rate in Los Angeles shot up in the 1850s. At one point, the town had a murder a day, according to historian Nat Read, in a population of not even 1,700. As Read points out in comparison, the Los Angeles crime statistics for 2006 (his book's date) had approximately the same murder rate (one a day) but in a population of over 3 million. At that 1850s per capita rate, one would think that the town would be depopulated in no time. But the continuing supply of drifters from all areas belied that possibility. For a while, Los Angeles' violent notoriety was unsurpassed. Even the celebrated "Wild West" towns of Dodge City, Abilene and Deadwood weren't this bad. In the morning, Angelenos would ask one another who got shot/knifed/murdered the night before.

One new Angeleno from Germany wrote a memoir of his early days in the pueblo, *Sixty Years in Los Angeles*, which has become a basic reference for what is known about the time period. Harris Newmark arrived in Los Angeles in 1853, where he became a store owner, trader and freight hauler. He made a fortune in real estate dealings. When he arrived, he found more than one hundred vineyards in the general area and seventy-five to eighty within the town itself.

## Mathew Keller (1811–1881)

Mathew Keller came to Los Angeles in 1851 after a long stay in Mexico. He was already known as "Don Mateo" from those years and easily fit in to the daily life of the still Spanish-speaking pueblo. Across the river was his good friend from the Mexico days, fellow Irishman, brother-in-law and vintner, Andrew Boyle. It didn't take long for Keller to rival Wolfskill and the Sainsevains in wine production. He built a home and winery at Alameda and Aliso Streets, with his first vineyard (twenty acres, with supposedly fifty-year-old vines, according to biographer Dinkelspiel) toward the river. He was constantly buying and planting new vineyards, famous for importing new grape varieties, and wrote a treatise on Los Angeles winegrowing in 1858 (Appendix 3). That report was sent to the U.S. patent office, along with a select bunch of grapes from his vineyards (that may have been a touch of his Irish humor; what condition were the grapes in upon arrival?). As at most other vineyards, the hard work at Keller's vineyard was done by the native Indians, many trained years ago at the missions. Keller appreciated their "art" with the vines. His large vineyard—150 acres—to the south of town was Rising Sun Vineyard, where he planted Malvoisie grapes as well as the ubiquitous Mission. Keller bought the Rancho Topanga-Malibu-Sequit, with its twenty-three miles of spectacular coastline, in the early 1870s (for ten cents an acre). The primary occupation was cattle ranching, but he began planting vines there (what he called Malaga Ranch, just above Santa Monica) a few years before his death, to the tune of five hundred acres.

Though he had become quite wealthy from his wine business (he was known as the "wine-making millionaire"), the national downturn in the economy during the 1870s coupled with accusations of poor quality of his wines substantially affected his income. He went to New York in 1877 to act as his own agent, writing that he went "to save my property and to get out of the wine business—and to do this I have risked my life in my old age in New York in the depth of winter to try and accomplish it…The wine business has been a millstone around my neck…It has swallowed up all I made on land

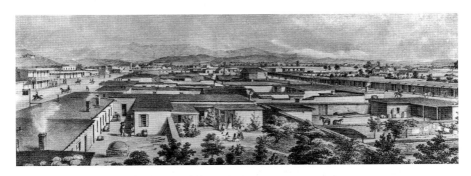

Kuchel and Dresel illustration of Los Angeles in 1857, view north and east. The large tree on the far right edge of the view is J.L. Vignes's El Aliso. *Courtesy of Library of Congress.*

sales and any other way." This was quoted by historian Thomas Pinney. His close friend in Los Angeles, the young German-Jewish shopkeeper turned banker Isaias W. Hellman, advanced him the money for his New York venture and maintained his business interests at home while he was away. In a few years, Keller was solvent once again and returned to Los Angeles.

Keller was an original investor and stockholder of the Farmers and Merchants Bank of Los Angeles, which was under the direction of Hellman. As a mark of his friendship and trust in the man, Keller appointed Hellman as executor of his will and guardian of his four children. Though Keller died in 1881, his estate wasn't settled until 1886, when all the children had reached their maturity (a stipulation of the will). For his probity, sagacity and honorable handling of his friend's estate, Hellman was universally commended.

## Kohler and Frohling

The chaotic growth of the wine trade in Los Angeles needed an organizing hand from the merchants' point of view, someone who could pull the disparate parts together and efficiently get the wine to the market in San Francisco and the gold fields. Two men played a key part in satisfying this need, and neither had any previous experience in winemaking, grape growing or business, nor had they even seen a vineyard. Charles Kohler, a violinist, and his musician friend John Frohling, a flutist, had both come to San Francisco in 1853 from their homes in Germany. Both met from their involvement in the Germania Concert Society, established to bring a sense of culture to the raw frontier town. But they could see that there was a great opportunity in the wine trade. Pooling their resources, they bought a vineyard in Los Angeles in May and harvested a first crop in the fall of 1854, with hired German help. Their first few hundred gallons sold out to their German and French clientele. As

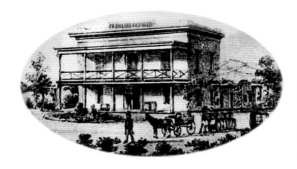

Kohler and Frohling's winery building on Main Street, circa 1857. From the Kuchler and Dresel illustration of the same year. *Courtesy of the Los Angeles Public Library Photo Collection.*

## A History from the Mission Era to the Present

the Americans caught on, their business grew by leaps and bounds. Dividing their responsibilities, Kohler remained in San Francisco as the salesman and organizer. Frohling went to Los Angeles to oversee the growing, harvesting and making of the wine. They were good at what they did, despite their inexperience. They bought grapes from every grower in town, with Frohling bringing his own crews to do the harvesting and crushing, which was fast and efficient. His winemaking methods and standards were far and away superior to what was being practiced at the time. By 1859, they were dominating the market in the pueblo, searching for whatever stock they could obtain. In that year, they made more than 100,000 gallons. The next year, they made so much they had to rent out additional space in the basement of the city hall. In 1861, they sent 130,000 gallons north. The Kohler and Frohling Co.'s appetite for more grapes to satisfy its market led directly to the founding of the Anaheim colony.

The company's next focus was opening an agency in New York. By 1860, it was doing so. It could not have been easy. With no road or train across the continent, sailing around the Horn of South America was the only way. Aging wine on a long ocean journey, however, was a tried-and-true method. The Sainsevain brothers also opened a New York branch in 1861. In this period, wine tastings in New York that advertised California wines were in actuality tasting Los Angeles wine, so dominant were the town's vineyards and winemakers. Shipments to New York and the eastern cities continued to rise. By 1867, 150,000 gallons of Los Angeles port, 80,000 gallons of Angelica (the Los Angeles specialty: a sweet, white-wine liquor) and 500,000 gallons of white wine from Los Angeles and Sonoma were shipped from California. The range of their wines indicate how far they had progressed from the Mission grape.

Kohler and Frohling played a dominant role in the continuing development of the California wine business (a role they had essentially invented). Frohling had died rather early on in 1862, but Kohler kept his friend's name on the business. When he died in 1887, he had helped change the state's rustic wine commerce into an industry, foreseen the importance of the northern vineyards and helped the shift to those areas. Years before, he had been cheerily prophetic, saying, "On the long run we will beat Europe anyhow." This amusing quote is from Thomas Pinney.

Angelenos were well aware of the importance and increasing prosperity of their wineries and vineyards. A grape motif made its way onto the original seal of the city, where it has remained in some form to this day. A short-lived newspaper appeared in the last years of the 1850s, the title of which implied this overarching influence: the *Southern Vineyard*. It was not a farmers' newspaper and had a decidedly Democratic Party slant, says Newmark in *Sixty Years in Los Angeles*, though near its end it had become Unionist in its sympathies. It was ably edited by J.J. Warner, another vineyard owner and friend of Mathew Keller. Grapes and cattle were the prime occupations in Los Angeles in the 1860s, and from this source, other businesses thrived. A huge flood inundated the low-lying vineyards along the river in 1862, but in the years after that, a drought of long duration destroyed the Southern California cattle business. Wealthy men like Abel Stearns were ruined. Grape growing became more important than ever. Secretary of State William Seward visited Los Angeles in 1867 and gave a speech from the balcony of the Bella Union Hotel, the town's main (and relatively grand but for the fleas) hostelry. He made many California references, each being met with a warm response. Lastly, when he said that he had seen the vineyards of Burgundy but that the vineyards of California far surpassed them all, he was met with a thunderous, long-lasting ovation.

Another early French wine company in Los Angeles was Vache Freres. Brothers Emile and Theophile Vache opened a winery on Aliso Street near Alameda in 1860. They had joined their uncle, also named Theophile, who had previously emigrated to California and, in the 1830s, had opened a small winery and vineyard near Hollister (or what was to be that city). A third brother, Adolphe, soon joined them. By the early 1880s, they could see that vineyards in the city center were being forced out by new industries. They bought land far to the east of town in an area they called Brookside (now Redlands) and planted a large vineyard, keeping their Los Angeles location for a while longer. Brookside Winery became a household name in the 1960s and '70s, operated by the Vaches' grandsons. Theophile II and Adolphe returned to France in their old age, a habit many other French émigrés imitated. Emile stayed and is buried in Evergreen Cemetery in East Los Angeles, not far from his countryman and fellow winemaker Jean Louis Vignes. In the 1880s, Emile published a recipe for making Angelica, the sweet, white wine named for the town. A twenty-first-century winemaker found the recipe doing research and, with the old Mission grape vines she found on her property in the Santa Rita Hills AVA in Santa Barbara County, is now producing Angelica the Vache way.

Pelanconi house on Olvera Street (Calle de la Vina/Vine Street until 1877) had been the winery building of an early Italian immigrant winemaker, Giuseppe Gazza, who came to Los Angeles in the Mexican period. His partner was another Giuseppe—Giuseppe Covaccichi—whose Italianized name masked his Croatian origins on the Dalmatian coast of the Adriatic. Antonio Pelanconi, from Lombardy in northern Italy, arrived in 1853 and began working for the two Giuseppes, ultimately taking over the business and buying the building that bears his name. He married Isabel Ramirez, sister of an early vineyard owner and neighbor. Their son Lorenzo carried on the winemaking business, only giving it up to his mother and her new husband in 1877 so he could concentrate on grape growing in his large vineyard north of town. At the great curve of the Los Angeles River, just north and east of Verdugo Creek's outfall, he planted his grapes on land where Jose Maria Verdugo very possibly planted his first vineyard of San Gabriel mission vine cuttings sometime in the 1790s. Pre- and postwar housing now cover the vineyard, but the area is known as the Pelanconi neighborhood, with a park and street that commemorate the name.

The railroad that connected Los Angeles with San Francisco in 1876 increased the tempo of changes in the old pueblo that began with the

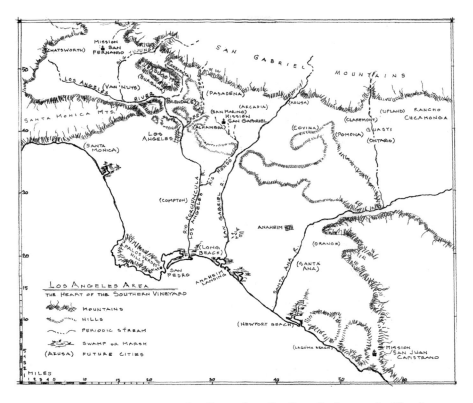

Map of the Los Angeles area from San Fernando to San Juan Capistrano, the "Southern Vineyard." *Map by the author.*

American occupation. It took the easiest route into the town: along the farmland next to the river—the prime vineyard land. As the vineyards and gardens began to go, so did the old zanja water system that irrigated them. New water pipes began to be installed, providing cleaner water to new homes and businesses. The old live willow tree fences that shaded narrow lanes were pulled out for housing and commercial uses. The once green swath that indicated the pueblo to approaching travelers out on the plain was decidedly less so. Vining plants that decorated flat-roofed verandahs on adobes disappeared when new, larger buildings took their place. With those flowering plants gone, the smells on the air changed as well. American-defined progress was arriving with each train.

## Chapter 5
# DEVELOPMENTS IN THE VALLEYS

## SAN GABRIEL

In 1854, Benjamin Wilson sold his home and winery on Alameda and Aliso Streets to the Sisters of Charity, a Catholic nunnery and educational organization. The 10-acre vineyard that went with it would provide the sisters with an income, as it had for Wilson. The crime wave in Los Angeles had become too much for Don Benito, now a former mayor. He had bought the 128-acre Huerta de Cuati in 1852, a portion of the San Gabriel mission property that had been given to Victoria Reid, the native Indian wife of Hugo Reid and a longtime resident of the mission. It contained a substantial vineyard itself, separate from the original two large, Mission vineyards, with some vines reputedly to have been planted in 1815. It also included half of the nearby lake just below the Old Mill in its canyon. He called his new place the Lake Vineyard Ranch. The road from his home skirted the lake to the north, ran up the canyon to the plain above and headed straight up to the mountains. It is known today in its truncated form as Lake Avenue, the major north–south street in Pasadena and Altadena.

The particular geography of this area of the valley is a small escarpment or drop in elevation from the alluvial-fan plain coming out of the Sierra Madre Mountains (now San Gabriels). The escarpment stretches from the Arroyo Seco in the west through the Rancho Santa Anita (now Arcadia) in the east. The natural declivities with spring water and oak woodlands that crease the escarpment attracted the native Tongva, the missionaries

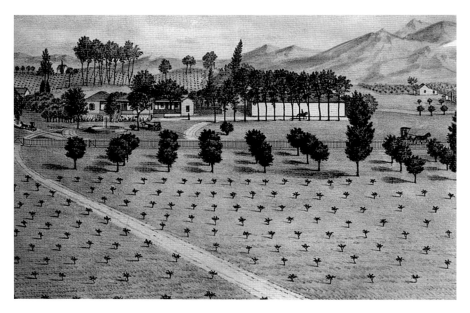

Drawing of the Benjamin D. Wilson place, Lake Vineyard Ranch near San Gabriel in the 1860s. *Courtesy of the Alhambra Historical Society.*

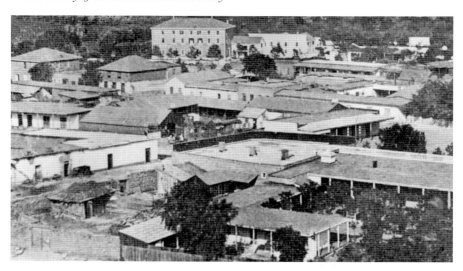

View over Los Angeles and the plaza area from the Pico House toward the Sisters of Mercy building at the corner of Macy and Alameda, circa 1875. Benjamin Wilson had owned the property from the 1840s, where he had built a house and planted several acres of vineyards. The winery and vineyard provided the sisters with an income to continue their work after Wilson sold it to them in 1854 when he bought his Lake Vineyard Ranch near San Gabriel. The vineyard can be seen surrounding the building. Hidden among the lower buildings in the foreground is the Pelanconi Winery, which is still extant on Olvera Street as La Golondrina Restaurant. *Courtesy of Los Angeles Public Library Photo Collection.*

and now Wilson, who saw its obvious agricultural possibilities as well as its beauty.

Don Benito moved in with his new wife, Margaret Hereford, and their children from previous marriages. He had already built a ranch house on the slope of the escarpment just to the east of his portion of the lake (on the slope above the intersection of Euston Road and Patton Place in what is now San Marino) and began planting more vineyards. There is evidence in his account books that he was experimenting with a champagne-style of sparkling wine in 1854–55, which "gives him the credit for producing the first sparkling wine in California," this from Thomas Pinney. He also planted fruit trees of all kinds, with a major grove of oranges. Ornamental trees lined his avenues, and his home became a showplace for visitors to Los Angeles.

Wilson was a major real estate force in the area, eventually owning most of the western San Gabriel Valley. He bought the Rancho San Pascual from owner Manual Garfias in partnership with Dr. John Griffin (the medical officer of General Kearney's invading U.S. Army of 1847) in 1859. The rancho became the cities of Pasadena and Altadena. He had an interest in the Rancho Ballona on the ocean, south of what would become Santa Monica. He had carved a road into the Sierra Madre Mountains to bring out timber from the slopes for his various purposes, including the making of wine barrels. The lasting result was to have the tallest peak named after him: Mount Wilson.

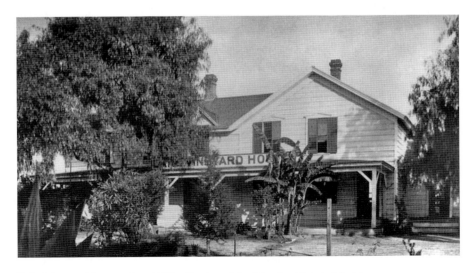

Lake Vineyard house, circa 1870s. *Courtesy of the Alhambra Historical Society.*

By 1860, his vineyards were over one hundred acres and increasing with every year. He had a San Francisco agent by 1862, and following the lead of Kohler and Frohling and the Sainsevain brothers, he obtained an East Coast agent in Boston in 1863. The demand in San Francisco was so great that he dropped the agent there and opened his own establishment in 1865. As with many other vintners who had agents on the East Coast and elsewhere, finding an honest one was key, as adulterated wines were the bane of the California winemakers.

What grapes did he plant? Like most of his neighbors, he had the ubiquitous Mission to start with. Then he experimented with Carignane, Zinfandel, Grenache, Mataro, Trousseau, Burger and Folle Blanche. But the sweet fortified wines of port, the celebrated Angelica from almost all Los Angeles vineyards and sherry were his standard products.

## JAMES DE BARTH SHORB

Just as the complexities and hardships of the wine business were weighing him down with its burdens, Don Benito had a young visitor as a guest in his

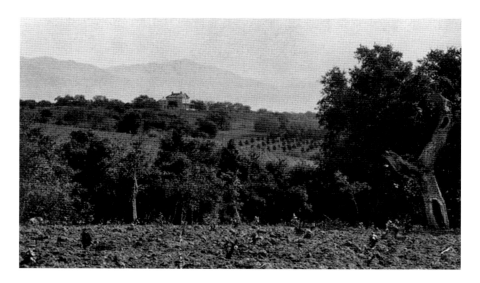

Lake Vineyard view east to the James De Barth Shorb family home on its promontory, with views of the valley and its own vineyards. When Henry Huntington purchased the property, he tore down this building and built his own mansion on the same spot. *Courtesy of the Alhambra Historical Society.*

home. So smitten was the young man with Wilson's eldest daughter, Jesusita (Sue), that very soon they were married (1867). James De Barth Shorb was the energetic partner Wilson needed to help him run the business, and their vision for that became one and the same. Shorb, born in Maryland, had arrived in California in 1863 at age eighteen, looking for oil in Ventura, with only $700 dollars to his name (as he said later). Possessed with a great amount of confidence to match his energy, he was determined to do all that the developing culture of wide-open Southern California had to offer. His career manifested his multifaceted interests. Exuberant and flamboyant by nature, he was a fluent talker and writer. Proud to be a "southern gentleman" and wishing to do business only with "gentlemen," the Catholic father of eleven children wasted no time in promoting the continued expansion of Wilson's wine business. He leased all his father-in-law's vineyards and cellars under the name of B.D. Wilson & Co., an operation to which his father-in-law lent only his name. An inventory showed that at that time (1867), Wilson had a wine storage capacity of roughly fifty thousand gallons. Shorb began a program of expansion of these cellars and planting more vines. He thought he could direct those projects from a distance, while operating the San Francisco agency. But the expansive plans for the vineyard brought him back. Requiring more workers for the new vines, Shorb brought in Chinese laborers in 1869, and he was the first to do so in Southern California. "He found they could be trusted to work alone after only a few days' instruction," according to Thomas Pinney. It was a successful move, one emulated by Shorb and Wilson's neighboring vine growers.

Shorb continually sought new markets for B.D. Wilson & Co., developing agents in New York, Chicago, Detroit, Baltimore, Cleveland and other cities in the East. At one point, the agent in New York was the winemaker/agent from Anaheim, the peripatetic Benjamin Dreyfus. Shorb also attempted foreign markets in South America, Mexico and Europe. As a Catholic layman, he cultivated altar wine contracts with the Archdiocese of Los Angeles.

By 1875, his hard work was paying off as the annual production of Lake Vineyard was 150,000 gallons of wine and 116,000 gallons of brandy, attested to by Thomas Pinney. Shorb was boasting that the company was the largest wine manufacturer on the Pacific coast and—in his opinion—produced the best wines in the state. Yet the difficulties of the business (dishonest agents, adulterated wines, shipping problems, low profits, etc.) would also prompt him to sell out from time to time. In that same year, he unsuccessfully attempted a sale of the firm's inventory: 80,000 gallons of wine, 7,000 gallons of brandy and the 30,000 gallons at the New York agent.

Shorb's energy and drive pushed him into other activities. He ran cattle and raised wheat on the Lake Vineyard property in the style of any good ranchero of old. The produce from the large citrus orchards was packed and shipped widely in the country, in tandem with the vineyard business. He had interests in mining in the Mojave, Arizona land and water developments and especially railways, which he saw as an indispensable part of the growth of Southern California. He was a force in Democratic politics, as well as in the vineyard and winery associations of the state. But it was land and water development that absorbed most of his interest.

## Alhambra and Pasadena

Don Benito had bought property early on to the south and west of his home, calling it the Lake Vineyard Extension. Together with Shorb, he began preparing the land for sale as a new community. Instead of digging open-water ditches (zanjas) to supply each lot acreage, Shorb developed an iron-pipe irrigation supply system from Wilson's Lake to reservoirs to each property. It was a significant step forward: the first subdivision with piped-in water. Wilson's daughters, Annie and Ruth, were reading Washington Irving's *Tales of the Alhambra* at the time and suggested that name for the new town. The first land parcels went up for sale in 1875 and sold out in two years. One can still see the water development work of Wilson and Shorb, with its often Byzantine nature of water rights in play. Deep in Kewen Canyon on the border between Pasadena and San Marino, the traveler will come upon a puzzling sign hanging on the fence surrounding large water tanks. It reads, "Property of the City of Alhambra."

In the fall of 1873, Judge Benjamin Eaton (Wilson and Shorb's neighbor to the far north) was hosting a land agent from Indiana on his Fair Oaks ranch and vineyard. D.M. Berry was the purchasing agent for the California Colony of Indiana, a group of hopeful immigrants from Indianapolis. Berry thought he had found the "promised land" for his investors in this part of the Rancho San Pascual and approached its owners. Earlier in the year, Griffin and Wilson partitioned the remaining portions of the rancho between them. Now Griffin wanted to sell his 4,000 acres to the Indiana group; Wilson wanted to keep his 1,600 acres but would sell to the Indiana group later. The sale was completed in late December, and on January 24, 1874, the shareholders gathered on the plain to apportion the land, each to receive 15 acres per share. To the west of the dividing line (now Fair Oaks Avenue), 1,500 had been surveyed and platted. Two years later, Wilson's land to the east was sold. Historian W.W. Robinson said, "By the end of May, the colony had houses, a reservoir to hold 3 million gallons of water, an irrigating system, 80 acres of grain raised for hay, 100,000 grape cuttings set out, 10,000 small trees purchased for nursery planting and a large area of land prepared for corn." Evidently the shareholders reached back to their Midwest roots for a name for their settlement, ignoring any local derivation: Pasadena, from the Chippewa language, meaning "valley between hills."

## San Marino

Don Benito had given land to the east of his Lake Vineyard Ranch to his daughter Sue and her husband for vineyards and a home site. In 1877, Shorb built a splendid house for his large family in the prevailing Queen Anne style of

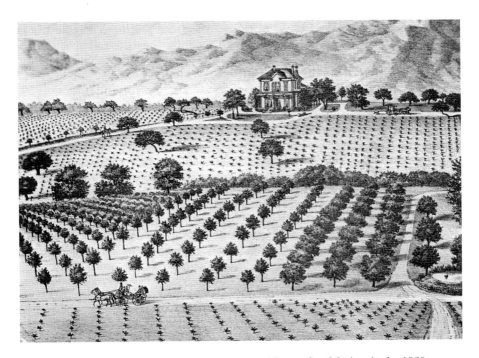

Drawing of the James De Barth Shorb property and home, San Marino, in the 1860s. *Courtesy of the Alhambra Historical Society.*

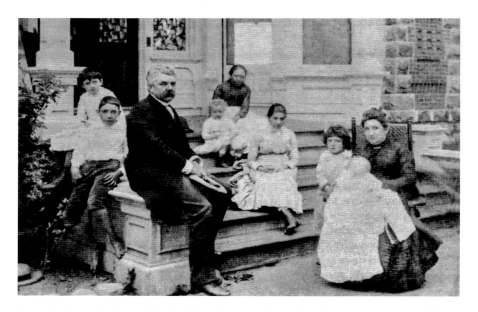

James De Barth Shorb and his family on the steps of their San Marino home, circa 1880s. Shorb had built an ornate Victorian mansion on a bluff overlooking the vineyards he had planted with his father-in-law, Benjamin Wilson. It was a showplace for the time, and it still is in its current reincarnation as the Henry Huntington Home, Library, Gardens and Museum. *Courtesy of the Alhambra Historical Society.*

architecture, on the brow of the hill overlooking the valley to the south, with its miles upon miles of vineyards and citrus orchards. It became a local showplace and focus of lavish hospitality for visiting dignitaries. Shorb called it San Marino after his grandfather's plantation in the Catoctin Mountains of western Maryland. Henry Huntington bought the property in 1903 and constructed his palatial home in the same spot, where it today enjoys the same view over the valley as the centerpiece of the Huntington Art Gallery and Botanical Gardens.

Benjamin Wilson died in 1878, and Shorb withdrew the winery from the market, selling his grapes in bulk to other wineries in the area. But he began planning what was to become the largest winery ever attempted in the state.

# L.J. ROSE

To the south and east of the Lake Vineyard Ranch was the Sunny Slope Winery and vineyards of Leonard J. Rose and his wife, Amanda. It became a

# A History from the Mission Era to the Present

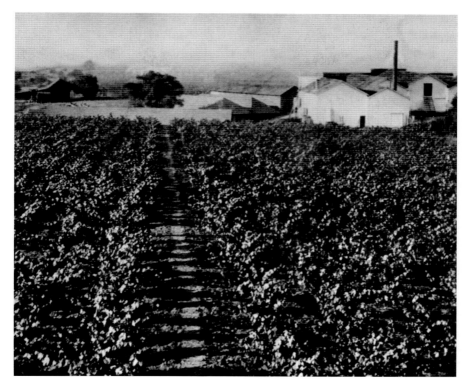

Sunny Slope Vineyards and Winery near San Gabriel, circa 1870s. *Courtesy of the Alhambra Historical Society.*

major player in the Los Angeles wine business, ultimately extending over one thousand acres of vines, with a brick winery of a 500,000-gallon capacity. Rose was born in Germany and came west in a wagon train, narrowly avoiding massacre by native Indians. He bought a portion of the Rancho Santa Anita in 1862, built a home (still standing on La Presa, just below Huntington Drive and east of San Gabriel Boulevard) and began laying out vineyards. He made use of the old dam site on the property, built by Joseph Chapman to hold water and power a mill at the San Gabriel mission. The dam exists as of this writing on the headquarters of the Sunnyslope Water District, the inheritors of the water rights of Rose's winery.

Rose planted the requisite Mission grape, which was used to make their Angelica. He planted Zinfandel and Black Malvoisie for red table wine, Blaue Elben and Burger for white wine and a smattering of Muscat. He also made a brandy. Like Shorb, he, too, employed the Chinese as laborers. In

1879, he began his grand expansion of the winery in response (like so many other California vintners) to the void in French wine production, created by that country's phylloxera destruction of its vineyards. In the mid-1880s, noticing the damage done to the vines of Anaheim by its mysterious disease and a partial infestation of his own vineyard, Rose sold his winery business to a consortium of British investors. Though Rose profited from the sale, the British group ultimately lost out. It caused foreign investment in Southern California vineyards to virtually dry up.

Thereafter, Rose continued with real estate investments, creating the communities of Lamanda Park (a contraction of his first initial and his wife's name), which became a center of wine and citrus production, and Rosemead. Lamanda Park was ultimately annexed by Pasadena.

The sale of the Sunny Slope Winery in 1887 happened in a very fortuitous year to do so, as it coincided with the extraordinary frenzy of a land boom in the Los Angeles area. Cheap train fares brought thousands of people to Southern California, where prices of land skyrocketed. E.J. "Lucky" Baldwin, a major landholder and promoter, was typical when he said, "Hell, we're selling the climate! The land we're giving away." Property was bought and sold at such a rate that it made people's heads spin. One new landowner, looking at the scrub vegetation of his new property, said to the agent, "What am I going to raise on this?!" The agent replied, "Why, raise the price to the next buyer."

The publication the next year of Helen Hunt Jackson's best-selling novel *Ramona* was a sensation and caused a renewed—but mainly romantic—public interest in the mission period. Business owners took advantage of this nostalgic dream, often twisting the actual facts out of proportion. L.J. Rose Jr., in the biography of his father, relates an example of this fabrication. A tavern owner in San Gabriel, abutting the old mission, had a huge grapevine shading the patio of his restaurant. On it he posted a placard that read: "This vine was planted by Father Serra in 1771." Not only was the mission not even there yet at the time, nor were its extensive vineyards not planted until much later, but L.J. Jr. also derisively writes that the vine was originally a cutting from one planted by his father in 1863.

Life along the escarpment was extraordinarily attractive to the new American immigrants. It seemed to presage an almost dreamlike way of life, a veritable fairyland, in the phrase of that time, meaning a place blessed. With its views south across the valley and back up to the steeply rising Sierra Madre Mountains, the area appeared to these new settlers as an idyllic pastoral scene. Soon Don Benito had many neighbors who began their own vineyards and citrus orchards, as he had done. Most of these grape growers sold their grapes in bulk to Wilson, Shorb, Rose, Baldwin or to the other wineries in Los Angeles. Just to the west, and owner of the other half of the lake, was Colonel E.J.C. Kewen, a lawyer, California attorney general and later Confederate cavalry officer who purchased the Old Mill of the padres in 1859. He planted grapes and is now mostly remembered for the canyon and road named after him. Union cavalry general George Stoneman (and later California governor) had been stationed in California earlier in his military career and had dreamed of returning. He bought a large ranch and developed both a vineyard and citrus groves, calling it Los Robles for the oak-studded hills. A major street in Pasadena has that name, as its southern end once stopped at Stoneman's property. It would have been interesting to be a "fly on the wall" to those political discussions of these neighbors of Northern and Southern sympathies. Michael White had a small vineyard east of Wilson, and still farther east was the 1,740-acre portion of the Rancho Santa Anita bought by Alfred Chapman, who also planted grapes and citrus. Chapman, a West Point graduate, had come to Los Angeles in the 1850s, resigned his army commission and studied law with Jonathan R. Scott, marrying his daughter. Later, he began a separate law practice with a boyhood friend from their native state of Alabama, Andrew Glassell. Their specializing in land titles with the old Californio rancheros became so influential that they caused the "Great Partition of 1871" of the Verdugo Rancho San Raphael. The resultant split parceled out land to many other important vineyard owners in the Southland, such as Prudent Beaudry, Ozro W. Childs, Benjamin Dreyfus of Anaheim and Chapman's own father-in-law, Jonathan Scott. Near Anaheim, Chapman and Glassell laid out an agricultural development called Richland Farms, which eventually became the city of Orange. In east Pasadena, the Chapman Woods residential neighborhood is named for him.

## Rancho Santa Anita

The original vineyard grower on the escarpment was Scottish immigrant Hugo Reid. Arriving in Los Angeles in the 1830s from South America, where he had business interests, he started his own *tienda* (supply store). A meeting with a Tongva Indian woman—Victoria Bartolomeu—left him smitten. He converted to Catholicism, taking the baptismal name of

Perfecto, and married Victoria after her first husband died of smallpox. He also adopted her four children. Not fascinated only by his wife, he was also equally fascinated by her Tongva culture, which was rapidly dying out from the ravages of European diseases. Don Perfecto (as Reid liked to be known) wrote a series of letters describing Tongva culture that appeared in the *Los Angeles Star* newspaper in the year of his death of 1852.

As a naturalized Mexican citizen by his marriage and conversion, Don Perfecto could own vacant land. In 1839, he laid claim to the 13,319-acre Rancho Santa Anita, carved out of the secularized mission San Gabriel lands. He received provisional title in 1841 and full title in 1845. As a condition of title, Don Perfecto had to build a house, raise a certain amount of *fanegas* of wheat (a Spanish unit of measure) for the public weal, raise cattle and plant a vegetable garden. An attractive feature of the rancho was a shallow lagoon near the escarpment, where Reid built his flat-roofed adobe with verandahs. To further bolster his title, he stated that he had planted ten thousand grapevines, presumably from cuttings acquired at the mission. It was the beginning of a constantly expanding vineyard by Reid and future owners, easily watered from the lagoon.

Don Perfecto sold the rancho in 1847 to his friend, neighbor, business partner from South America days and fellow Briton, Henry Dalton. Unfortunately, Dalton had his hands full defending his immense landholdings elsewhere in the San Gabriel valley and neglected what Reid had started. After a few more short-termed owners, William Wolfskill bought the rancho in 1865. He began expanding the vineyard and citrus orchards and planted from seeds the first of a new tree from Australia: eucalyptus. When Wolfskill died the next year, his son Louis continued the work of vineyard expansion and agricultural experimentation. Rising land prices encouraged Louis to sell off parts of the property, and in 1872, he sold the remaining 8,500 acres to Los Angeles businessman Harris Newmark for $85,000. Newmark had experience with vineyard property, having bought the Vejar family holdings just south of the pueblo, and continued its vineyard and winery business for several years. But he could see the further rise in land prices that the coming railroad would bring. When Elias J. Baldwin offered him a generous $150,000 just three years later for the rancho, Newmark countered with $175,000. Irritated, Baldwin refused. But after a time, he agreed to the price. However, Newmark informed him that the price was now $200,000. The shocked Baldwin finally agreed to the new price. It was the largest real estate sale up to that time in Los Angeles County. Newmark was not an easy mark.

## A History from the Mission Era to the Present

Elias Jackson Baldwin (1828–1909) arrived in San Francisco in 1853 from Ohio. He made a quick fortune in mining stocks in the Comstock Lode in Nevada, where his adroit moves gained him the nickname "Lucky." Much later, he came to Los Angeles to investigate rumors of gold mining in the Big Bear Lake area and passed through the rancho. The beauty of the place and his ability to see its future promise determined his purchase of the rancho. He immediately began developing its agriculture: new groves and orchards, experimental nurseries, new irrigation schemes and buying water rights. The already large vineyard of the Wolfskills expanded yet again to a massive extent. The huge vineyard can be seen on a map/survey of the rancho prepared in the late 1880s, extending from what is now Santa Anita Avenue on the east to Michillinda Avenue on the west, all above today's Huntington Drive. This roughly four-mile-long area includes all of the Santa Anita Racetrack and its mammoth parking lot, the Santa Anita Golf Course, the Santa Anita Mall and its large parking lot and the residential neighborhoods to the west of Baldwin Avenue below the Los Angeles County Arboretum. He built his own brick winery building to hold the annual production of 384,000 gallons of wine and 55,000 gallons of brandies of Baldwin Distilleries. He obtained wine merchant agents in New York and San Francisco. The winery building is still standing, on the hill overlooking the west turn of the Santa Anita Racetrack, slightly obscured by a line of those eucalyptus trees started by William Wolfskill so long ago.

## San Fernando

In 1845, Governor Pio Pico leased the San Fernando mission and its lands (the valley) to his brother Andres, who was to gain fame two years later as the general of the Californio army that checked the invading American army at the Battle of San Pasqual in eastern San Diego county. Despite already having an adobe of his own nearby, Andres Pico moved in to the old mission buildings, making what would soon be a well-known hospitality center for miles around, where days-long fandangos (dancing and socializing parties) were a way of life, long a tradition among rancheros. Where the distance between settlements was immense and the population small, simple communication meant a many-hours-long horseback ride to the intended ranch house. Friends and family would gather at a certain hacienda and stay for days at a time, discussing events and conducting business. Hospitality—formal and informal—was supreme.

Pico repaired some of the buildings and continued the great twin "gardens" started by the padres some forty-five years previously. He had added new vines to the existing missionary stock, as was implied in a report of 1858. Andrew McKee, a journalist from San Francisco, visited Andres Pico's mission hacienda and included his observations in a treatise on "The Grape and Wine Culture of California" sent to the U.S. Patent Office:

> *At the mission of San Fernando, twenty two miles north of Los Angeles, can be seen the gardens, inclosed* [sic] *with high adobe walls, embracing 54 acres, containing forty two thousand grape vines, one hundred pomegranate trees, three hundred peach trees, ten apricot, ninety orange, five cherry, and twenty two fig trees; but the place is chiefly remarkable for its beautiful grove of four hundred large olive trees in full bearing.*

If the report is accurate, Pico had almost doubled the amount of vines that were extant at secularization in 1833. He continued the mission tradition of wine and brandy making, selling it to the miners in the goldfields. His brandy was particularly well received.

Farther south of the mission, along the western slope of the Verdugo Mountains in the sandy, alluvial loam that is just right for grapes, Jonathan Scott began planting an extensive vineyard in 1862 on his property that he had traded with Catalina and Julio Verdugo, sister and brother owners of the Rancho San Raphael. Scott had arrived in Los Angeles in 1849 from Missouri. He became the first American justice of the peace and administered the first oath of office to the first American City Council of Los Angeles on July 3, 1850. Scott had originally bought the 5,745-acre Rancho La Canada in the high, mountain valley above the Verdugo's rancho but had exchanged that acreage for 4,603 acres on the west side of the San Raphael. Clear title was only to be had after the "Great Partition" of the Rancho San Raphael in 1871 to satisfy all the claimants and lien-holders of the property. Julio and his sister Catalina had divided the rancho between themselves in 1860, allowing Julio to borrow money to finance a new dwelling and agricultural activities on his portion. He had planted a large vineyard on one-hundred-plus acres of his property to the west of his new adobe on what is now Verdugo Boulevard and Acacia Street in southern Glendale. He defaulted on the loan—which had usurious rates and conditions—which caused the "Great Partition." Interestingly, the lion's share of the rancho (8,424 acres)

## A History from the Mission Era to the Present

went to Benjamin Dreyfus, the storekeeper, grape grower and wine merchant of Anaheim.

Scott's vineyard and winery operation began a winemaking business tradition that continued for over one hundred years in what is now the Burbank area. Scott did not stay long and sold his landholdings in 1867 to a New England dentist immigrant, Dr. David Burbank, who merged Scott's acreage with his own Rancho Providencia, just to the west. From this nucleus came the future town named for the immigrant dentist founded in the great land boom of 1887. Burbank kept the vineyards that Scott began, though his main focus was on sheep ranching. A photo of the little village in the 1880s shows a huddle of buildings surrounded by large vineyards.

## CUCAMONGA

Tiburcio Tapia, the original grantee of the Rancho Cucamonga, died in 1859. His daughter and her husband, Maria and Leon Victor Prudhomme, sold the 13,000-plus acres to John and Maria Merced Rains. Rains and his wife had been living with her father, Isaac Williams, on his Rancho del Chino farther south in the valley. Now they began cattle and sheep ranching on their new property on the alluvial-fan plain below the towering peaks

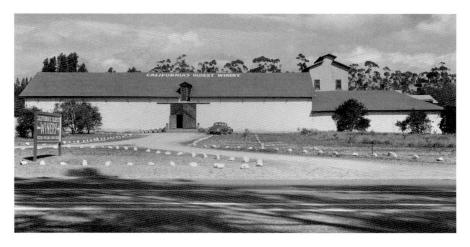

The old Cucamonga Winery (seen in this photo from 1939) went through many names and owners since the first vineyard was planted on the property by the first owner, Tiburcio Tapia of Rancho Cucamonga, in 1839. *Courtesy of Los Angeles Public Library Photo Collection.*

of the Sierra Madre (now San Bernardino Mountains) and adding vines to those already planted by the Tapia family. In a few years, Rains had put in 160 acres of vines, making wine and brandy, much of this work with the help of the Sainsevain brothers. Tragically, Rains's tenure of the rancho was short. In November 1862, he headed out to Los Angeles for business but was ambushed and shot. His murderer was never found. His wife, Maria Merced, remarried, but the rancho came on hard times. It was sold at a sheriff's sale in 1870.

The buyer was Isaias W. Hellman. He quickly sold off several thousand acres and formed an investment consortium with his one-time mentor Governor John Downey, O.W. Childs and his cousin Isaiah M. Hellman to subdivide the land for agricultural purposes. Keeping the vineyards started by Tapia and Rains, he employed a longtime friend and winemaking associate, Jean Louis Sainsevain, to restore the neglected vineyard and add to it. Within a year, another forty thousand vines had been added, and Sainsevain was making port, brandy and Angelica (Sansevain Street in Alta Loma and Sansevain Peak in the San Bernardino Mountains were named for him and his brother, Pierre). For a time, the Rancho Cucamonga was one of the largest vineyards in the state. In the not-too-distant future, a neighboring district with its sandy soil would house the largest vineyard in the world. Hellman maintained his connection to the rancho property in one form or another right up to Prohibition. Hellman Avenue in Alta Loma (Rancho Cucamonga) commemorates his name, just as Hellman Avenue from Alhambra through Rosemead commemorates his name in the San Gabriel Valley.

## Isaias Wolf Hellman (1842–1920)

Isaias Hellman is an often-overlooked figure in the wine history of California. To do so is to diminish his undeniable importance and miss his crucial significance in funding the wine businesses of the state, particularly those of Los Angeles. His relationships with many of the winery and vineyard owners—first in Los Angeles and then later up and down the state—enabled those enterprises to thrive. Though never a winemaker himself, his intimate knowledge of that work was gained from his close friends (especially Mathew Keller), vintner associates and investments in vineyard property. His steadily increasing influence in the development of California was mainly due to his land and other banking investments, which caused him to move to San Francisco in 1890. His interests in the wine business of the state continued, and he gained control of the powerful—near monopolistic—California Wine Association. Either ironically or serendipitously, he died at the inception of Prohibition, not living to see the destruction of the California Wine Association and the state's wine industry that he had so assiduously cultivated for all of his life.

Born into a German-Jewish family in Reckensdorf, Bavaria, he and his brother Herman immigrated to the United States. Arriving in Los Angeles in 1859 at seventeen years of age and virtually penniless, he began working in a cousin's dry goods store; by 1865, he had his own. From his store, he got into banking almost as an afterthought. He had an ad-hoc system of safety deposits for his customers. After an altercation with one of them, he realized he had better formalize any further arrangements. It was then that he began using banking deposit slips, buying customers' valuables and equipping his organization with the trappings of a real bank.

At the time of his purchase of the Rancho Cucamonga, Hellman was getting married and founding the Farmers and Merchants Bank in Los Angeles. Some of the original stockholders included Mathew Keller, John Downey and O.W. Childs. In a population of just over five thousand in 1870, Los Angeles was a close-knit community. The bank was long-lived, avoiding ruinous (or ill-starred) lending practices that destroyed others (i.e., Workman and Temple Bank) to become a force in financial dealings throughout the state. Many grape growers came to rely on loans from Hellman, and many other Southern California business enterprises—now considered fixtures—owe their beginning support to this bank.

So important did the Farmers and Merchants Bank become that Hellman almost single-handedly stopped the financial panic of 1893 in Los Angeles from spiraling out of control. In that year, the nationwide economy slumped as a whole. Customers of many Los Angeles banks began a run on their deposits, resulting in bank closures. With a population increasingly frenzied to get their money back, Hellman showed up at the train depot, boldly unloading sacks of gold coins (well guarded) onto waiting wagons in front of a crowd of onlookers. Slowly, the wagons made the trip to the Farmers and Merchants classically designed bank building, with the crowd following. On the long, mahogany bank counter, Hellman directed his tellers to stack the coins in what came to be called by news reporters "towers of gold" for all to see. With this nonchalant show of confidence and strength, the panic receded, and a banking collapse was averted.

Hellman and others saw the need for a university in Los Angeles and (with the "usual suspects"—Downey, Childs, Keller, etc.) helped to found the University of Southern California in 1880. He was also appointed to the board of regents of the University of California, along with Leland Stanford, in an attempt by the university to attract students from wealthier families. However, in an obtuse political move, the governor fired them both. This so angered Stanford that it ensured that his fabulous fortune would not be going to the university. Instead, he founded his own. Less troubled by this turn of events, Hellman persevered and was reappointed by a later administration. His financial association with Stanford continued when that railroad tycoon began pouring more of his fortune into a huge vineyard and winery operation in the far northern county of Tehama in the Sacramento Valley.

Even after his 1890 move to San Francisco—the state's center of gravity for population, finance and the burgeoning northern California wine industry—Hellman was still closely involved in Los Angeles businesses. He was a major proponent and stockholder of the mammoth San Gabriel Winery operation of James De Barth Shorb. When that business foundered (on overextension, a national downturn, Shorb's death and vine disease), he had the sad—but inescapable—duty of foreclosing on Shorb's widow (Sue Wilson, daughter of Don Benito Wilson) and taking her to court in 1899. Hellman was involved in the founding of several streetcar lines over the years, including that of the Pacific Electric line of Henry Huntington. It was at the urging of Hellman and George Smith Patton (Shorb's brother-in-law, neighbor and lawyer) that Huntington bought the widow Shorb's foreclosed estate—San Marino.

The Cucamonga Winery, started by Tiburcio Tapia in 1839, went into other ownership after Hellman's death, continuing—until recently—as the Thomas Winery. It claims to be the oldest continuously run winery in California. The old buildings and winemaking paraphernalia are still there at the corner of Foothill Boulevard and Vineyard in Rancho Cucamonga.

## Phylloxera

In the early 1870s, news began filtering into California about a disastrous calamity befalling the great vineyards of Europe, specifically those of France. A disease of unknown origin with no known cure was steadily moving through the French vineyards from its start in the south around the Rhone River mouth. Vineyard owners there had noticed that vine leaves had withered and dropped, and the fruit never ripened. Within three years, the vine was dead. But there was nothing to see when the root was pulled up, as the pest had moved on. By 1866, the disease had spread so much that farmers were voicing their concerns, alerting the agricultural authorities. One of the large vineyard owners—Gaston Bazille—contacted the head of the pharmacy faculty at Montpellier University, Jules-Emile Planchon, who had a major interest in entomology. Meeting at a vineyard close by in the summer of 1868, Planchon, Bazille and other scientists dug up an infected vine and inspected the roots. With the aid of a magnifying glass, they could see the entire root system covered in a tiny mass of insects, each no larger than a pinprick, making the vine seem painted in yellow. Planchon recognized the insect as being similar to *phylloxera quercus*, which causes leaf galls on oak trees. He named the new insect *phylloxera vastatrix* (the "Devastator") after looking at the huge expanse of dead and dying vines. Still the cause was unknown, with many thinking the little insects could not possibly kill vines by themselves and that it must be a weakness in an otherwise healthy vine.

When the disease showed up in the Bordeaux region, worry became more widespread than before. The Societe d'Agriculture of the Gironde offered a prize of 20,000 francs for an effective cure. Suggestions poured in, mostly absurd or useless. But two lines of serious research began to emerge: elimination of the pest and finding a vine immune to its attack. It was found that flooding a vineyard with water would drown the insect. But that required an absolutely flat vineyard. Very few fit the bill, and those were not the vineyards of quality grapes. Vines in sand were found to be immune to the disease, but that also posed problems. Soil fumigation held out some hope as it did kill off the insect—and sometimes everything around it, including the vines and endangering the humans by the noxious chemicals with their explosive natures. That danger and its great expense militated against a widespread use.

As the disease continued to spread, it became more imperative to find a vine that was immune. Simple logic said that if the disease came from Europe, then vineyards would have been wiped out long ago. From many different scientists involved came the idea that perhaps a foreign grapevine might be immune. Some native American vines appeared to be phylloxera-proof. Since it was the root of the French vines that the pest attacked, perhaps grafting a French vine cane onto the American rootstock would solve the problem. American vines had been imported hundreds of years before but rejected because of their "foxy" taste. If a graft was done, would the foxiness transfer into the French top? While these ideas were debated, Planchon conferred with an American entomologist, Charles V. Riley. An Englishman by birth and educated in Europe, Riley had immigrated to America virtually penniless. By virtue of his polymathic interests, he had risen to become the chief entomologist of the state of Missouri. Famous in scientific circles for his work on the Colorado beetle in which he had used a "biological warfare" technique to eradicate that threat, Riley wrote an influential paper on the phylloxera danger. He confirmed what Planchon had suspected: phylloxera was an American native insect pest, living on its host grapevine without killing it. In sailing ship days, the insect had not survived the months of a sea voyage. But now in the age of steam, months had been turned into days, with the insect surviving to conquer a whole new continent. Riley had been one of the first to suggest grafting vinifera vines onto American rootstock, and his wide authority had a special gravitas. But not all American vines were phylloxera-proof. Which ones were? Which ones would take to the different European soil? In their continuing communications, Riley referred Planchon and other French scientists to the vineyardists and horticulturalists of the German immigrant community of Hermann, Missouri. They had made a thriving winemaking business out of the native American grapevines, conducting extensive tests and experiments. Under the direction of George Husman, a horticultural professor, friend and colleague of Riley's; Hermann Jaeger, a Swiss immigrant horticulturalist; and Isidor Bush, an Austrian immigrant nurseryman and winemaker, the vineyard owners of Hermann sent "millions upon millions of American cuttings and vines," according to Husman, writing in 1880, to the French scientists and vineyard owners for trials from 1873 to 1876. Years of laborious breeding and grafting programs followed to discover which would do what on what ground. Many old varieties of French grapes were lost during the period because of their inability to graft or because they had died out before the grafting program had come along. But this process saved the French wine industry from extinction, a possibility that had stared it in the face. That wine would be just a footnote in the future history of civilization was unthinkable to the French.

The phylloxera continued into all the other wine-producing countries of Europe: Italy in the early 1870s, Spain by 1878 and France's colony of Algeria—thought to be the savior of the mother country's winemaking—by 1885. Austria-Hungary and the Balkan countries were ravaged as well. In most of these areas, with their livelihoods destroyed, immigration to the Americas seemed the only way out for many. The historic wave of immigration to the United States from the late nineteenth into the early twentieth centuries was caused in part by the phylloxera epidemic.

Regardless of the danger and opportunity for other winemaking countries of Europe, "France was the world's biggest producer and consumer of wine by such a margin that whatever happened to her industry affected everyone. Up to 1870 she had been a net exporter by a proportion of 8 to 1. By 1880 she was a net importer by 3 to 1, and in 1887, at the height of the crisis, imported 12 million hectoliters and exported two," according to Hugh Johnson in his *Story of Wine.*

Just when it seemed that the native American rootstock would be the salvation of the French wine industry, a new vine plague broke out in France that overshadowed the phylloxera. Riding along in the American root cuttings was a powerful new form of mildew. It was called "downy" to distinguish it from the "powdery" mildew that had attacked the French vineyards in the decade before the onslaught of phylloxera. With this third disease in thirty years, the Golden Age of French winemaking of the 1830s through the 1850s seemed but a distant memory. But within four years, the famous "Bordeaux mixture," a combination of copper-sulphate and lime in liquid form, provided the cure.

In California, vineyard owners and winemakers looked on the disaster in France as an opportunity. Many wineries geared up for large exporting possibilities to France and made eminently sensible projections to their bankers and financiers about wine sales in Europe to fill the void of French wine. Perhaps the prophecy of Charles Kohler was now going to come true. Despite the excitement of new markets, California winemakers overlooked one thing they had in common with France. Though many considered the Mission grape a native-to-California grape, it was still a vinifera grape and vulnerable to phylloxera attack. The pest arrived in Sonoma in the early 1870s with large importation of native American vines from the East and Midwest, just as it had in France. As it began its steady march through the vineyards in the north, growers seemed unconcerned, even ignoring the warnings coming from Professor Hilgard at the University of California. But soon enough, diffidence turned to worry, and eradicating the pest became a prime motivation for the creation of the Board of State Viticultural Commissioners in 1880. When the pest appeared in the south of the state, the almost pure sand soil of the Cucamonga Valley protected the vines, just as the French discovered in their attempts to combat phylloxera. Because of this area's apparent "prophylaxes," it attracted new plantings. After producing 48,000 gallons of wine in 1870, Cucamonga was producing

279,000 gallons in 1890, according to Thomas Pinney. Cucamonga reached its apotheosis with the huge vineyard and winery production of Secondo Guasti in the early twentieth century.

## Chapter 6

# ANAHEIM

## *Episode on the Santa Ana*

The story of the Anaheim agricultural colony is a fascinating one. It started with high hopes and a great organization, moving from strength to strength to a seemingly bright future. But a catastrophic and mysterious vine disease caused its total annihilation after only thirty years of existence.

By the mid 1850s, Kohler and Frohling realized that the demand of their San Francisco business would ultimately exhaust the wine capacity of the Los Angeles vineyards if they could not add more to the supply. They began casting around for a solution. Bay Area vineyards had the population center close by but were in their infancy, had very few useful vine cuttings on hand and could not be expected to provide what was needed for years. Los Angeles, though farther away, was the center of their business, had an immense store of vine stock on hand and was located on the wide and fertile empty plain just south of town. The solution lay in that direction: new vineyards on a large scale.

Who would do the work? Early on, Kohler and Frohling's main clientele were their German countrymen. They had listened to their stories of immigrant loneliness and disillusionment with the wild, violent society they had encountered in San Francisco. Forming an agricultural colony with the numerous Germans of San Francisco seemed the solution for this part of the plan. Kohler and Frohling brought in another German-speaking associate, former deputy surveyor for Los Angeles County George Hansen, an Austrian immigrant. He was to set up the organization, manage the operation and figure out the myriad details. The first meeting with the interested Germans took place in February 1857. With the colony plan explained, the Los Angeles Vineyard Society came into being.

The plan had a corporate setup. The society would issue fifty shares at $1,400 each. The shareholder would receive a twenty-acre parcel of land, of which eight acres had to be planted as a vineyard. To secure a share, a participant had only to make a down payment and pay off the rest through installments. By then, the land would be ready for him. The society now had the wherewithal to prepare the land for its occupants, and the shareholder could stay employed.

Hansen, as general manager, began looking for property along the Los Angeles River, south of town, but nothing panned out. A previous survey client who lived along the Santa Ana River wanted to sell, so in September 1857, Hansen purchased a 1,165-acre tract with water rights from Juan Ontiveros, owner of the Rancho San Juan Cajon de Santa Ana. Hansen hired a team of Indians who laid out the irrigation system and the main water canal from the river six miles away. The street grid in the original section of Anaheim reflects the northeast–southwest orientation of those early gravity-flow water ditches (zanjas). Willow and alder poles (like those in Los Angeles) were driven into the ground around the perimeter of the settlement, which would grow into a live fence protecting the vines and gardens from animals out on the range. The 20-acre lots were laid out and the vines planted on each property: 400,000 Mission grape cuttings (at 1,000 per acre), mostly from William Wolfskill's Los Angeles vineyard. After two years of work and $60,000, Hansen was ready for the shareholders.

At a meeting a year earlier, the society members had decided on Anaheim (barely beating out Anagau) as the name for their new settlement. These Germans were a diverse cross-section: they came from all areas of Germany, were Protestant and Catholic and were tradesmen and mechanics. What united them was their shared German culture and a sense of purpose to prosper out on the wide plain, raising their families in a peaceful rural life. All but one had never farmed. But the tasks of grape growing and winemaking were their overriding concern.

Each shareholder was an independent winery, in competition with his neighbor. In the first decade, there were forty-seven wineries. The first small harvest brought 2,000 gallons in 1860. Four years later, production was up to 300,000 gallons, rising to 1,250,000 gallons of wine and 100,000 gallons of brandy twenty years later. Over the years, the original settlers had drawn more eager immigrant vineyard owners to the surrounding countryside, and now those vines were adding to the production. By 1883, the total vineyard

## A History from the Mission Era to the Present

acreage in the Santa Ana River valley was estimated at 100,000. Anaheim wine soon was everywhere in the state, particularly in the gold fields, where it was highly regarded. The success of the vineyard society was manifested in the large and gracious homes built by the settlers and their ever-increasing capacious wine cellars.

As was the purpose of the Vineyard Society, most of the wine went to Kohler and Frohling. The wine barrels from each of the wineries were loaded on wagons, brought to the Anaheim Landing (currently at Seal Beach, just south of Alamitos Bay) on the coast and transferred to small boats that would drive through the surf to waiting ships anchored out in the roadstead. The ships would make the voyage up the coast to San Francisco and unload into the company's cellars. Years later, a long pier and wharf out into the ocean were added to make the transfer much less arduous.

The vineyards and their owners had to endure the rigors of living on a dry, somewhat desolate plain. Low, scrub plants alternating with grasslands covered the dry hills in the distance to the east. The only shade trees were those that the colonists planted themselves to shield themselves from the long, hot summers. With regular intensity, Santa Anna winds swept across the basin, blowing out of the deserts, and funneled through that river canyon. Anaheim sat directly in the path of those ferocious winds. Winter brought the rains, and they were rarely predictable, ranging from minimal to torrential downpours. In the flood year of 1862, the water in the streets of Anaheim was so high that the inhabitants had to scramble for their lives to higher ground in the hills. The rain had started on Christmas Eve in 1861 and didn't let up for three weeks. For almost a month thereafter, the entire plain was an inland sea. In February, the Los Angeles, San Gabriel and Santa Ana Rivers all merged to form a massive river "mouth" from Long Beach to what is now Huntington Beach. The vines in Anaheim sat caked in mud, as recorded by Harris Newmark in his memoir.

Despite these setbacks, shops and other businesses expanded in the town. The first (arriving even before the society members) was Benjamin Dreyfus, a Bavarian Jew who foresaw the possibilities of the new community and opened a store in 1858. His success was such that he eventually established his own winery, making wine from his 235-acre vineyard. He had gone to San Francisco in 1863 to be the agent for the Anaheim winemakers (leaving a manager on his Anaheim property), where his operation expanded to include other wineries and an office in New York. He had land in Cucamonga, San Gabriel and San Fernando Valleys (part of the Rancho San Raphael) and Napa. He even made kosher wine.

With the success of the Anaheim colony, the rigors of the original pioneering years gave way to more ease and grace. By the late 1870s, rough shacks were displaced by large multistory homes and mansions placed on lush, manicured grounds. The sun-baked water ditches became shaded by *allees* of mature willow trees. Continuing financial and community development seemed assured.

But in 1883, workers in various vineyards of Anaheim noticed a strange mutation on the vine leaves. It reoccurred the next year and the one following, each time more extensive and with deepening severity. It signaled a new change that was about to fall on the grape growers, one that would end their existence as vineyard owners.

*Chapter 7*

# RISE OF THE NORTH

The amount of vineyards and winemaking in the lands around San Francisco Bay in 1848 was minimal at best. Outside of the old mission vineyards of San Jose and Santa Clara at the south end of the bay and San Rafael and Sonoma in the north, growers were few and far between. One of the first was George Yount in the Napa Valley. Nearby in Solano County was John Wolfskill, brother of William, and a friend of Yount from their trapping days. General Mariano Vallejo had taken over the miniscule Sonoma mission vineyard (about three hundred square feet, according to Sir George Simpson, visiting in 1842) and had augmented it with further plantings. The Wolfskills had brought vines and cuttings from Los Angeles and the San Gabriel mission. There were a few more grape growers in Sonoma and a handful in Santa Clara.

After the first frenzy of gold mining retreated, sensible men looked around for a more stable way of living. As it has been said, those who supplied the miners were the ones who made the fortunes. Agriculture was no exception. With the influx of population from all over the world, a diverse group of experienced winemakers had arrived. They began planting new vineyards in some of the old mission areas and searching for new places and new grape varieties that would grow well there. The French immigrant growers of Santa Clara County were the first to plant these new varieties. Pierre Pellier had brought vines with him from Bordeaux in 1852. Louis Prevost had over sixty varieties, while Antoine Delmas had imported ten thousand French cuttings and was taking prizes for his wine. By 1858, Delmas had a vineyard of 350,000 vines of 105 different varieties, according to Thomas Pinney. German, English, Dutch and American immigrants all fanned out into the counties surrounding the bay, out around the Sacramento area and into the foothills of the Gold Country. They looked in wide wonder at the beauty of the California countryside, seeing the tremendous potential for agriculture. They all realized that California could be the "vineyard of the world" and proceeded to plant vines on an explosive scale. By the end of the 1850s, from having virtually no wine production at all in 1848, the north was well on its way to becoming a serious competitor with the south.

The wine production census of 1860 shows a total of 246,518 gallons produced in the state that year (Pinney states that the figures are probably too low). Los Angeles produced 162,980 gallons, San Bernadino and Santa Barbara Counties produced 19,000 gallons and San Francisco Bay and Mother Lode Counties produced 64,000 gallons. Statewide vine planting estimates were equally impressive: 1,500,000 in 1856, 2,265,000 in 1857 and 3,954,000 in 1858. Though the north was planting at a furious pace, Los Angeles alone doubled its plantings in the same period, so Thomas Pinney attests.

## Agoston Haraszthy

Because the California wine business was young and untried, many winemakers were inexperienced and tended (in the case of American immigrants) to fall back on methods that were useful in the eastern states (ie., Ohio River vineyards of native grapes) but ineffective or ignorant in California. Standards and criteria were fluid, to say the least. In 1860, the Committee on Wines of the State Agricultural Society wrote, "Most of our people have never seen a vineyard. Whoever will enlighten [them] on the most approved modes of agriculture, and, above all, the scientific and practical treatment of the grape juice in the making of wine will be a great public benefactor."

A remarkable man had appeared on the scene whose actions, speeches and writings went a long way toward providing that enlightenment. Agoston Haraszthy, Hungarian by birth, had arrived in the Bay Area by way of Wisconsin and then San Diego, where he had been elected county sheriff in 1851. Later in the same year, he was elected again to the state legislature in Sacramento. He never returned to San Diego and abandoned the vineyard he had planted there. Two more vineyards that he planted on the San Francisco peninsula met with failure. Looking around for a better vineyard area, he found it in Sonoma. He bought 560 acres in 1856, adjacent to General Vallejo's vineyards, and immediately began planting vines. After a year, he had fourteen thousand imported vines of 165 varieties. By 1858, this number had grown to 280 imported varieties. His Chinese workmen dug long cellars into the mountainsides, and Haraszthy built a Pompeiian-style villa, which he named Buena Vista. His sons had vineyards of their own, and one son was sent to France to study champagne making. He also planted extensively for other local grape growers, such as Krug, Bundshu and Gundlach. By the end of 1857, he was personally responsible for the tripling of Sonoma County vine acreage; he claimed to have the largest vineyard in the state.

A man this bold and energetic soon caught the attention of state agriculture officials. The California State Agricultural Society asked him to write an article about scientific grape growing. His "Report on Grapes and Wine in California" appeared in February 1858 and was widely disseminated in the state. In it, he castigated the dominance of the Mission grape and recommended the art of blending, among other points. In 1861, he was appointed by Governor John Downey to a commission to assess ways to improve and promote grape growing in California. His charge was to travel to Europe (at his own expense) to observe winemaking and vineyard techniques in the major areas of the continent and report them to the state. Traveling first to Washington to obtain introductory letters and then to New York to arrange for a book deal, he sailed for Europe with his family on July 13. Arriving in Paris, he first visited the Burgundy region and then went into Germany, buying up vines as he went. Next, he traveled into Italy—Turin and Asti—but not Rome or Naples. He then went back to France and the Bordeaux region and then across the Pyrenees into Spain. From Madrid, he went to Malaga on the south coast and Alicante on the east. He went back to Paris, and after a stormy crossing of the Atlantic to New York, he arrived in California by December 5. He made a brief report to the state in January 1862, saying that California had more "natural advantages" than Europe and urged the state's involvement in plant exploration, an experimental farm and elimination of wine fraud. His book came out in short order: *Grape Culture, Wines and Wine-making, with Notes upon Agriculture and Horticulture*. Over the years, it has been hailed as a monument in the literature of winemaking. Thomas Pinney is rather dubious about that distinction (and the man's legend) for good reasons. It is sketchy at best on European techniques, more travel writing and self-aggrandizement than agriculture. But it is important as a first exposition of a California winemaker to receive nationwide attention.

Haraszthy was indeed a natural-born promoter, with seemingly inexhaustible energy, always promoting California wines (especially his) across the country. When his stock of 100,000 vine samples arrived in 1862, he had three hundred varieties or so. He began selling them around the state and asking to be compensated for his European expedition expenses. The state legislature said no, citing the terms of his commission. Interestingly, the zinfandel variety does not appear in his vine collection from Europe. Part of the Haraszthy legend is that he brought that variety to California. But as Thomas Pinney points out, it had already been a favorite of East Coast enthusiasts since the 1830s and was planted in California as early as the mid-1850s. Zinfandel went on to be the most planted variety in California.

In 1863, Haraszthy sold all his lands to the Buena Vista Vinicultural Society, a corporation with the aim to be the largest winemaker in the state, with himself at the helm. Quarrels among the stockholders ensued, and accusations against Haraszthy's management forced him out. He left the country and died a mysterious death in Nicaragua in 1869. His real legend is his grand vision for the future of California wine, tirelessly promoted with his outsize personality, supreme confidence and apparently superhuman energy. He did more in ten years at Buena Vista than many in a lifetime.

## Boom and Bust

Vineyard acreage expansion continued at a fast pace in the 1870s and '80s. Boom and bust cycles were the norm through the state, some coinciding with severe economic downturns in the national economy. But several factors were occurring that favored the growth of the north over the southern vineyards. Wine production in each of these areas was virtually equal in 1870. By 1890, the north was out-producing the south in gallonage by almost five to one. Figures for the north were from the East Bay Counties, Santa Clara in the south and Napa, Sonoma, Solano and Yolo Counties to the north of the bay. Figures for the south were Los Angeles County alone.

In 1869, the cross-country railroad was completed, linking San Francisco and the gold fields to the major cities of the East. Wine shipments to those markets now had a direct, shorter transport time than the old shipments that would take months going around the tip of South America. From the opposite direction came another increase in population, with new growers and winemakers.

The singular topography and climate of northern California created a more temperate growing zone than that found in the south. The coastal mountains running northwest by southeast had gaps that allowed cooler air (and fog) to be drawn into the mountain valleys from the ocean, whose very cold currents originated in the Gulf of Alaska. The "manager" of all these air currents was the huge, hot plains of the Central Valley. The broken-up geography of the lands surrounding the Bay Area created what came to be called—in a much later time—microclimates, eminently suited to grape growing. In Southern California, the unique east–west mountains of the Sierra Madre (San Gabriel/San Bernardino Mountains today) above the wide-open plains of the Los Angeles Basin and its inland valleys next to warmer ocean currents created a much more uniform climate zone with less rain and longer, hotter summers influenced by the great deserts to the east. To achieve cooler temperatures in this area, one had to plant vines at higher elevations along the mountain front, which was difficult to do on those steep, crumbling slopes.

In an age of slower travel and communication, agricultural areas lying close to the centers of population, wealth and power had greater advantages than those farther away. The rising influence of the wine merchants of San Francisco (such as Kohler and Frohling) led to the creation of the California Wine Association (CWA) in 1894, after a particularly bad economic downturn combined with a period of vineyard overproduction. Its near-monopolistic power dictated grape pricing, what was grown and sold and how it was done for the next twenty-five years. It provided stability and growth for its members. Becoming profitable, controlling influence soon passed to its banker, Isaias Hellman, who had financed many vineyard and winery operations up and down the state. The headquarters building in San Francisco had huge storage cellars in its basement, where wine was blended according to CWA standards, creating a uniform brand and taste. However, the ten million gallons of wine in storage was lost in the San Francisco earthquake and fire of 1906. One eastern winemaker described it as "one of the greatest calamities that ever visited the California wine business." Had that wine come to market, it would have made the reputation of the state, as Thomas Pinney opines. But CWA recovered, and its power and existence was broken only by the advent of Prohibition.

The education of grape growers and winemakers took a major step forward with the almost simultaneous creation of the California Board of State Viticultural Commissioners in 1880 and the appearance of Eugene Hilgard as dean of the College of Agriculture at the University of California–Berkeley. Both were concerned with the advancement of quality winemaking in the state, and they frequently quarreled on what (and who) was the best way to accomplish that. Both were alarmed at the spread of phylloxera infestations in the Bay Area vineyards (it appeared only sparingly in the south), especially with the phylloxera epidemic destroying the vineyards of France and Europe at the same time. California winemakers had been poised to take over the world of wine, with the crushing disaster occurring in the French vineyards. Now it was happening to them; the dominant grape variety in California was still the Mission, and it—after all—was vinifera. Hilgard summed up winemaking problems in an article that appeared in the *San Francisco Examiner* on August 4, 1889 (though he might have exaggerated to make a point):

> *The poor quality of the larger part of the wines made and their immaturity when put on the market* [were part of this problem]…*The foreign guest at our principal hotels might be aghast at having the claret cork fly at him, followed by a significant puff of smoke, and a liquid resembling sauce rather than wine and of uncanny odor.* [The California winemaker] *after promiscuously crushing grapes sound, moldy, green and sunburnt…allows his fermenting tanks to get so hot as to scald the yeast, and then wonders why the wine has "stuck"; permits the "cap" to get white with mold and swarming with vinegar flies and then cheerfully stirs it under so as to thoroughly infect the wine with the germs of destruction.*

Hilgard set in motion the meticulous—and now immense—research in viticulture and enology that is the hallmark of the world-renowned University of California–Davis (originally the experimental farm of Berkeley) and its equally important cohort at Fresno State University.

*Chapter 8*

# DECLINE IN THE SOUTH

The 1880s opened with the southern vineyards overtaken by the north in vineyard plantings and wine production. The seven Bay Area counties, where the main growth was occurring, were together slightly one-third more in land size than the single Los Angeles County (which still included what would become Orange County) in the south—the prime growing area. Los Angeles was still adding vineyards and opening new wineries, just not at the same explosive rate as the north. At this time, the Central Valley was also planting vineyards at a rapid rate, whose aggregate acreage—more than fifty years later—would dwarf both the north and the south.

The newly formed Board of Viticultural Commissioners included two members from the south: James De Barth Shorb, member at large, and L.J. Rose, representing the southern district. The other representatives of the eight-member board were dominated by northern interests, especially by its president, Arpad Haraszthy (son of the indefatigable Agoston), and Charles Wetmore, the board's own dynamo and public face.

In Los Angeles, new immigrant winemakers—especially from Italy—continued to maintain the very diverse lot that was the original. Giovanni Piuma arrived at this time, opening a winery on Main Street near the Plaza that only closed in the 1940s. He had vineyards in the El Monte area. The De Mateis family had a winery in the older section of Los Angeles and vineyards in San Gabriel and later in Cucamonga.

Just to the south of downtown, Remi Nadeau, a former mayor of Los Angeles, bought land in the area known as Florence. A French-Canadian, he had made a fortune as a freight hauler and investor in eastern California silver mines. In the early 1880s, he began planting two thousand acres of vines, including the (de rigueur) Mission, Malvoisie and the ever-popular Zinfandel. He built a large winery complex but committed suicide in 1887 at the height of the land boom. The housing tract mania of that time rolled over his vineyards. His name is remembered in the area with Nadeau Street.

## Georges Le Mesnager

Georges Le Mesnager and his business partner Pierre Durancette were in the wholesale liquor and wine business in the early 1880s when they built their first winery, Sunny Side, at Second and Los Angeles Streets. Le Mesnager (difficult for American tongues past and present to pronounce: some say Luh Mess-na-shay, others Luh Mezz-na zhay or Luh Menna-zhay) had come from Mayenne, France, where his family owned vineyards. He arrived in Los Angeles (by certain accounts) in 1866. He most likely worked for the winery of his countrymen, Vache Freres, on Alameda, as he very prominently invoked its name in his later advertising. Later, the Vache brothers moved east and opened the Brookside Winery (in what is now Redlands), at the same time as Le Mesnager's new Sunny Side Winery was opening (Le Mesnager had several wineries under a variety of names). When the Franco-Prussian War broke out in 1870, Le Mesnager went back to fight for France, becoming a color-bearer. A patriotic Frenchman despite his long life in Los Angeles, he vowed to fight again for France should the need arise. He became prominent in the French community of Los Angeles, edited a French-language newspaper and gave a fiery speech (in French, of course) at the centennial celebration of the French revolution in 1889. He felt that France needed him again in 1914, and he returned to his home country to become famous as the oldest soldier in the French army (either sixty-four or seventy, depending on birthdate believed). He was wounded, returned to Los Angeles and then went back again to France as a liaison officer on General Pershing's staff. He returned once more to Los Angeles and finally back to his boyhood home, where he died in 1923.

In 1883, he was advertising for all sorts of wine bottles at the corner of Los Angeles and Commercial Streets. In the same year and same location, he later advertised that he had on hand over 100,000 gallons of wine of all types. He invoked Vache Freres and mentioned the "House established

# A History from the Mission Era to the Present

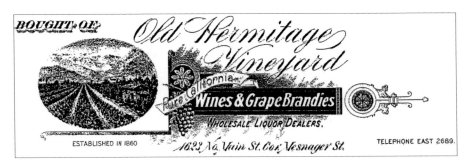

Letterhead/invoice of Le Mesnager Winery on North Main Street, Los Angeles, using the signature "Old Hermitage" brand. Some of the letterheads included "successors to Vache Brothers." The 1860 date implies that reference to the start of the Vache winery. *Courtesy Historical Society of the Crescenta Valley.*

1860," the year that the Vaches opened their first winery. Georges would use that year repeatedly on his stationery.

As a winemaker in Los Angeles, he (and his partner, Pierre, who evidently was very low key, compared to the effervescent, boastful Georges) began buying vineyard property, primarily in the northern part of Verdugo Canyon. There is some evidence that he purchased a vineyard from the Sainsevains in what is now Rialto in the Cucmonga area. In 1886, he purchased over 700 acres on the high slopes of the San Gabriel Mountains at the mouth of Dunsmore Canyon in La Crescenta. He now had reportedly almost 1,300 acres in vines in the Verdugo/La Crescenta area. Later, the Le Mesnagers were joined by other winemakers, making the old Rancho La Canada lands filled with small-property vineyards.

In 1893, his business was raided by Los Angeles tax collectors for not paying his liquor taxes and letting his liquor license lapse. From a new winery site on North Main Street, his son Louis took over the business and continued making and selling wine. At one point, they owned Anacapa Island to run sheep.

Louis is the one who started developing the ranch buildings on the high La Crescenta property. He began building the stone barn in 1905. By a series of building "campaigns" of stone work, it was completed in 1915 and still exists. Louis managed other family vineyard properties. They had a way station building and corral on Glendale Boulevard in Glendale, the halfway point where the horses were watered and rested on the trek down from Dunsmore Canyon to the winery in Los Angeles with the wagonload of grapes. Vineyard planting continued ever higher and farther into the canyon.

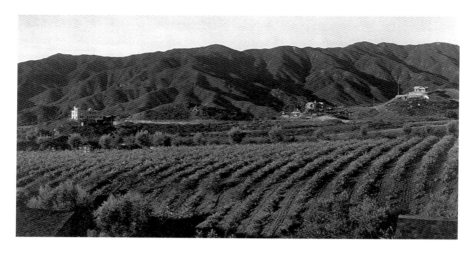

View north to the San Gabriel Mountains of vineyards in the western La Canada valley about 1910. On the left is Lieutenant Governor Wallace's castle, later notoriously known locally as the "Pink Castle" after the lieutenant governor's angry wife painted it that color. *Courtesy Glendale Public Library.*

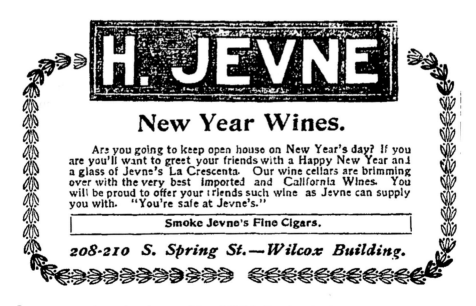

Jevne grocery store advertisement (circa 1898) in Los Angeles for La Crescenta wines. Hans Jevne was a Norwegian immigrant grocer who set up retail stores at the same time as George Ralph of present-day Ralph's grocery stores. *Courtesy Historical Society of the Crescenta Valley.*

A History from the Mission Era to the Present

The lower part of the vineyard is at 2,200 to 2,500 feet elevation, while the flat "banks" of land along the creek in the farthest reaches of the canyon range between 2,700 and 3,000 feet. It was one of the higher-positioned vineyards around. Georges's grandson Louis Jr. always maintained that his father's best grapes were grown there. What they were is still a mystery.

Another Crescenta/Canada ranching family was the Halls, who started a winery and planted vines in 1884. It turned into a sizeable operation when tourists in horses and buggies from the resort hotels in Pasadena started arriving for wine-tasting parties. Shipments to the east resulted. However, the main business was selling in bulk to Los Angeles wineries, which continued after the winery was closed down in 1904. Appropriately enough, the ranch was on Winery Canyon. Almost all of the far-flung vineyards in this high valley supplied the wineries and store owners in Los Angeles, even through the 1960s, when urbanization overwhelmed them.

## James De Barth Shorb

After the death of his father-in-law, Don Benito Wilson, Shorb seemed to put the wine business on hold, preferring bulk sales from his still-producing vineyards to merchants in San Francisco, such as Benjamin Dreyfus and others. Dreyfus, the dominating presence in the Anaheim wine area, also had an outlet in New York. He owned properties in Cucamonga and San Gabriel and had a large claim on the recently divided Rancho San Raphael of the Verdugo family. It was a natural thing for winemakers in the south to ship their wine by train in bulk to San Francisco for reshipment to the markets in the East. A direct rail link had not yet reached Los Angeles.

Bulk wine shipments were not without their cost. Shipping rates based on tonnage were coupled with taxes on wine shipments. If one could ship only the grape "must," the tax could be avoided, and the weight of wine could be reduced by taking out the water, or so the reasoning went. Shorb jumped into this business (among many others) but found it bedeviling. It took precious time and money away from the project that was to dominate the rest of his life.

Shorb was planning a new winery project on a grand scale. He wanted to build an operation large enough to compete on the world market and solve some of the vexing problems of California winemaking in the process. The analysis leading to the formation of the San Gabriel Wine Company was

# Los Angeles Wine

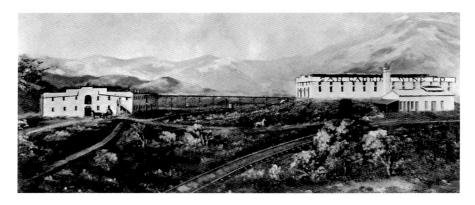

Painting of the huge winery buildings in Alhambra, built by James Debarth Shorb for the San Gabriel Wine Co. *Courtesy of the Alhambra Historical Society.*

sound enough: the vineyards of Europe were collapsing under the onslaught of the phylloxera vine disease and would soon be unable to supply their own demand; California vineyards had the capacity and quality (some said destiny) to fill that void; a company that controlled its product from vineyard to customer would solve the ubiquitous practices of fraudulent and adulterated wine sales; the company's land in the valley (and elsewhere) would be far more valuable when the proposed railroad link connected Los Angeles directly to the east. This solid logic attracted a range of very prominent investors mainly from Britain (where Shorb had been attempting wine sales for years), as well as the powerful California banker Isaias Hellman (a friend and fellow vineyard owner). With a fine prospect for the future, and heavily financed (though with not as much money that was ultimately needed), the company opened for business in 1882.

On its 1,500 acres, new vineyards were planted in each succeeding year, and arrangements were made to purchase grapes from surrounding vineyard owners (such as Sunny Slope, Hellman's Cucamonga vineyards and the new vineyards of the Sierra Madre Vintage Co., for example). The new brick winery buildings being constructed in Shorb and Wilson's new town of Alhambra had a fermenting capacity of 1.0 million gallons, with 1.5 million gallons of storage. But problems arose that worried investors. The sales end in the East had not yet been solved, and existing independent agents still had to be used. The company thought the majority of them were less than ethical. But many eastern merchants were dubious of the wine quality they were receiving, with some dismissing it as garbage. Both attitudes had some merit. The capability of the chief winemaker was in doubt. The company

# A History from the Mission Era to the Present

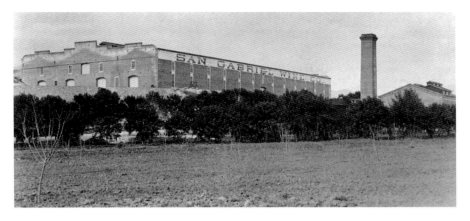

This 1880s photo shows the huge winery building for the San Gabriel Wine Co. in Alhambra. *Courtesy of the Alhambra Historical Society.*

became more reliant on its land sales, which were spectacular in the land boom of 1886 through 1887. L.J. Rose of Sunny Slope took advantage of the rise in real estate prices and sold his vineyards and winery to more British investors in 1887. The winery buildings that Shorb constructed (entirely of brick) presented problems of their own, as the interior—over time—was too hot and dry. The wine quality suffered. The company's indebtedness rose. Regardless, the sales kept climbing.

Just as things began to look better, the Anaheim disease came to the San Gabriel Valley. Shorb was quick to take action, using his status as a Viticultural Commission member to hire botanists to arrive at a solution. That would take time, something the company did not have. Shorb resisted the notion of bankruptcy and began to plant oranges as a way to stave off insolvency. This angered Hellman, a major stockholder of the company, who insisted it be allowed to go out of business and the assets divided. The constant worry and the continual demands of all the other enterprises with which Shorb was involved caused his health to fail. His doctor brother in San Francisco and his wife pleaded with him to take better care of himself. In 1890, he was in a precarious state: about to lose his business and his health, and his wife's inheritance from her father, Don Benito, was heavily mortgaged. In that year, he issued a report in his capacity as a Viticultural Commissioner on the Anaheim disease in the southern district: Anaheim was almost entirely wiped out; the San Gabriel valley had been seriously infected, but the disease was now passing; the Cucamonga valley and east had also been seriously affected, but there, too, the disease was rapidly passing; only the San Fernando valley was unaffected. Though the report was positive for future vineyard health (and perhaps somewhat disingenuous), news of the disease and the company's heavy indebtedness made the sale of the San Gabriel Wine Co. almost impossible. The land boom had passed, and prices had fallen. The United States went into a financial panic in 1892–93, which hit hard at all the state's winemakers.

Shorb and his wine company staggered along, selling what they could, often at "fire-sale prices." He died in 1896 after being confined at home for some time. He was only fifty-four. His business expired a few years later. The company had in its great winery at dissolution nearly 150,000 gallons of wine (95,000 in port; 25,000 in sherry, amongst other wine varieties), and 50,000 gallons of brandy. It still owned 1,170 acres of land. Shorb's attorney brother-in-law and neighbor, George Smith Patton, assisted in the breakup of the company. Hellman foreclosed on Shorb's widow, Sue, in an 1899 court case. Afterward, she moved (with her children) to San Francisco. Shorb and his children are memorialized in street names, the only visible reminders in the town of Alhambra that he and Don Benito created. The huge winery buildings passed into other uses and were torn down in the 1980s. A Target store (almost as large as the winery buildings) occupies the

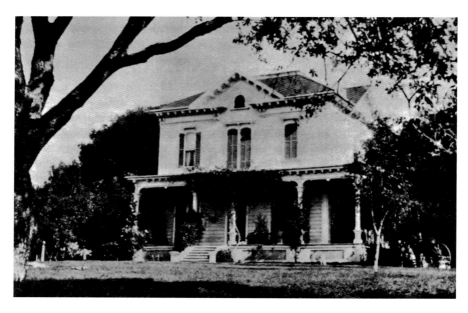

James De Barth Shorb house south elevation, circa 1880s. *Courtesy of the Alhambra Historical Society.*

spot at Main Street and Palm. A plaque placed near the entrance of the store by the Alhambra Historical Society commemorates the winery, the "largest in the world."

J. De Barth Shorb had been involved in so many pursuits and activities in the life of Southern California that it is difficult to describe. The ambition and energy that characterized his life had finally outstripped the ability of his health to accomplish them all. His personal legacy is the name "San Marino," his grandfather's plantation in Maryland. As legal heirs of the San Gabriel Wine Co., Hellman and George Smith Patton helped Henry Huntington to buy the vineyards and property in 1903. He had wanted to change the name to Los Robles but kept San Marino nevertheless. He built his own home soon after to house his growing art collection. Shorb's Carpenter Gothic home was torn down, and the great Neoclassical "palace" that is there now took its place, with its unobstructed view over the huge vineyard that was the San Gabriel Valley. But the bold vision (similar to Haraszthy's and others of similar character) of what the California wine industry could be is the true legacy of Shorb and his father-in-law, Don Benito.

# The End of Anaheim

The disease that had infected the San Gabriel vineyards came from just a few miles south of the valley in Anaheim. By 1883, the German winemaking immigrants with their fifty wineries were producing more than one million gallons of wine a year. Their success had caused more vineyards to be planted in the near vicinity, with new, independent settlements growing wine and raisin grapes. Workers began noticing a curious change on the vines, especially the Mission. The leaves looked "scalded," and the fruit would not ripen, withering in a soft mess. The next year, it happened again, only in an expanding area, and so on the next year. In its first years, the disease seemed not to have crippled the Anaheim vision of its future existence. Benjamin Dreyfus, the "wine king" of the area, felt confident enough to begin building a stone winery building, larger in capacity than any other in the neighborhood. But as the disease continued on its course, growers turned to the Board of Viticultural Commissioners for help, who hired a botanist to investigate and find a solution. The University of California got involved and began its testing, followed by the U.S. Agriculture department, the investigator of which was not particularly helpful. Regardless of that, the agency report estimated a $10 million loss for Anaheim and the Los Angeles area. The disease continued to spread, destroying almost all in its path, and no one seemed to know what it was or what to do. The agriculture department sent another investigator, Newton Pierce, who was much more methodical and scientific than the first, whose report appeared in 1891. He said that the "disease was none of those currently known, and that no remedies existed for it," as quoted by Thomas Pinney. He suspected that it was a bacterium but couldn't prove it with the methods and techniques of the day.

The disease was later named for him, and it is still a recurring problem today, especially in Southern California vineyards. By the time of Pierce's report, the great experiment in Anaheim winemaking was gone, reduced to only a few acres of barely producing vines. The stone winery building of Benjamin Dreyfus remained empty of wine. It went on to other uses, partly torn down for a freeway project and then completely demolished in 1973. The German immigrants planted their decimated vineyards with groves of oranges and other citrus, which soon was even more widespread than the vines ever had been. They also turned completely to their breweries, which they always had; working in the vineyards is a thirsty business. In turning away from their winemaking roots toward another fruit crop, they made a future statement in 1889 by seceding from Los Angeles County and forming Orange County.

As if to put a *finis* on the decline, the great sycamore—the Aliso—that had stood for centuries beside the river, long before it had stood in the yard of Jean Louis Vignes's winery, finally died. Before its end, the Philadelphia Brewery that had bought the land from the Sainsevains continued using the shade of the tree, too, for their customers' ease in the hot sun. But as the brewery developed, the one-story wood-and-adobe buildings gave way to multistory brick ones that wrapped around the tree on three sides. It meant cutting off many of the tree's limbs, weakening it in the process. After one branch fell and damaged some equipment, one of the brewery partners lopped off all the rest of the branches in a fit of pique. His other partner protested the desecration, but only a tall stump remained. By the end of 1892, it was dead. It remained in that condition until 1895, when an "experienced local axman" named William Willoughby chopped the tree down to be sold for firewood. The event drew a crowd, and people picked up chips and remnants as souvenirs of the ancient tree that had been a symbol for an era that had already changed beyond recognition.

*Chapter 9*

# TURN OF THE CENTURY THROUGH PROHIBITION

## LOS ANGELES IN THE NEW CENTURY

A newspaper article of September 3, 1905, appeared in the *Los Angeles Herald* listing the major sweet wine growers in Los Angeles and the Southland (Los Angeles, San Bernardino, Riverside, Orange and San Diego Counties), along with this particular statistic: "In 1904, 10,148 carloads of wine and brandy were shipped out of the state, of which 667 carloads were shipped from Southern California wineries."

The dominance of the Bay Area and the Central Valley winemaking areas was apparent, particularly the Central Valley, where bulk wine shipments were becoming the norm.

First on the list was the Sierra Madre Vintage Co. of Lamanda Park (now part of east Pasadena). Albert Brigden and his partner, C.J. Clark, had founded this vineyard and winery in 1885, planting over eight hundred acres adjacent to a large vineyard on the west started by Scottish immigrant James Craig in the 1870s. Just north of the Vintage Co. were three hundred acres of vineyards planted by Charles Cook Hastings in 1882. Unfortunately, Brigden died in an accidental explosion at his winery in 1894. But his Sierra Madre Vintage Co. became one of the largest vineyards and wineries in the San Gabriel Valley, lasting—and profiting—into the Prohibition era. The company employed a diverse workforce, especially Chinese, which can be seen in some of the surviving photos of the company. The workers planted

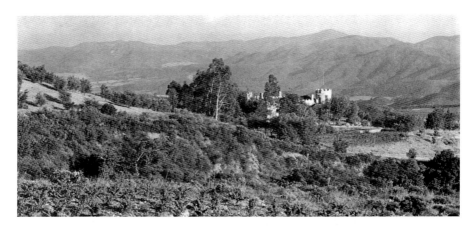

A photo of Gould Castle Vineyards showing the castle on its prominent site offering views of the valleys and the ocean out to Catalina Island and beyond, circa 1910. *Courtesy Glendale Public Library.*

zinfandel, blaue elbing and mataro grapes, among others. The company shipped its wines to the East Coast, as the winery was conveniently located on the main rail line.

Not mentioned in the list was the Golden Park Winery. Founded by brothers John and Peter Ettienne in the 1890s, with a winery complex at the corner of Allen and Villa Streets in East Pasadena, their vineyard was on part of the original James Craig vineyard property. They made red and white, sweet and dry wines; sherry; port; and brandy. The brothers were high profile in defeating several California state prohibition measures between 1914 and 1918. But with the Federal Prohibition Law in force, they closed the winery portion of their business in 1920. Part of their separate, second vineyard acreage now is occupied by Pasadena High School.

Also in the San Gabriel Valley were: Charles Stern and Co., the successor firm to the Sunny Slope Vineyards of L.J. Rose; Baldwin Distilling Co., Lucky's operation in Santa Anita; Jacob Rudel in San Gabriel; and August Steinke in Azusa.

In Los Angeles, the list included Giovanni Piuma, who had his vineyards in El Monte; Louis Le Mesnager (son of Georges), with vineyards in Verdugo Canyon and La Crescenta; Albert Rambaud, who also had a contentious lease on part of the Le Mesnager vineyard holdings in that valley; the Southern California Wine Co.; and Atalus Niemeyer. In the Garvanza section was the San Raphael Ranch Vineyard that had been started by Prudent Beaudry in 1875, conveniently located next to a small, spring-fed lake in the rolling hillsides.

# A History from the Mission Era to the Present

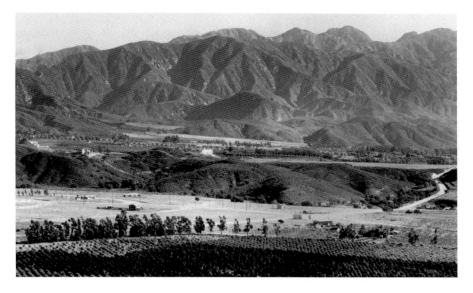

An early Montrose view (circa 1914) looking northeast of the vineyards and citrus groves in the valley and up to the tablelands of La Canada. *Courtesy Glendale Public Library.*

North along the river in Tropico was Giovanni Gai and, farther north, the West Glendale Winery; both had offices in Los Angeles. South of Los Angeles were Downey Vintage Co. on the old rancho of Governor John Downey, John S. Baker in Santa Fe Springs and Artesia Vineyard in Norwalk.

Even in the blighted vineyard area of Orange County, there were still five wineries in Anaheim and Orange: Tim J.F. Boege, William J. Fisher, George O. Rust, George Young and Joseph Young. Farther south in San Diego County, there were four wineries mentioned: Emanuelle Darien in Otay (on the Baja border), G.F. Merriam and Son in San Marcos, George C. Kuchel in Escondido and Louie Young in De Luz (near Fallbrook).

John McClure was listed as a winemaker in Shorb Station. He had bought the Ramona Winery, one of J. De Barth Shorb's spin-off properties south of the San Gabriel Winery complex in Alhambra. It was not McClure's first vineyard. He had emigrated from County Antrim, Ireland, and arrived in Los Angeles, where he was working at the dry goods firm of Dillon & Kenealy in 1875. In partnership with those gentlemen, he later planted a vineyard on 160 acres at the mouth of La Tuna Canyon near the settlement of Roscoe in the San Fernando Valley in the 1890s. It was a vineyard notable for its lack of irrigation; it relied on the natural flowing groundwater out of the canyon, and with that water source it was successful. He is most known

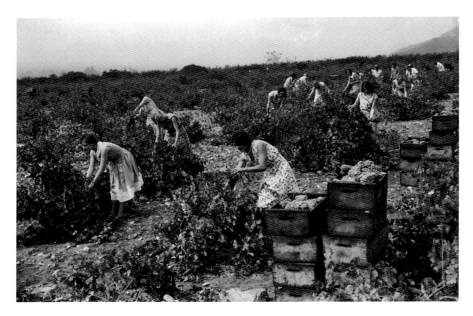

Burbank grape pickers on the slopes of the McClure winery under the Verdugo Mountains, circa 1910. *Courtesy of Burbank Historical Society.*

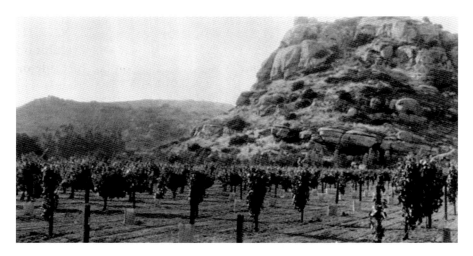

In the western reaches of the San Fernando Valley (Chatsworth) stands the great rock formation known as Stoney Point, part of a larger series of unique and dramatic rock hills at the Santa Susanna Pass. In the late nineteenth through the early twentieth centuries, a vineyard sat directly below the imposing stone outcrop. *Courtesy of the West Valley Museum.*

for his Sunnyside (or Burbank) Winery that he built on the one-thousand-acre purchase he made in 1900 in Burbank. On the slopes of the Verdugo Mountains, he planted three hundred acres of vines and constructed a modern winery. It was still producing into the 1940s.

Out on the west side of Burbank, the Brusso family—Italian immigrants from the north of Italy—planted a large vineyard in 1915, despite the fact that Burbank voted to become a dry city in 1914. They managed to survive and thrive in the face of that decree and the coming of Prohibition. Their vineyards encompassed many acres on Thornton and Ontario Avenues. Theirs was the last winery in Burbank to fall to housing tracts in 1969.

Neighbors of the Brussos were the Randisi family, who started their winery in 1906. It also lasted through Prohibition and the postwar housing boom. Its abandoned winery buildings, in the middle of a housing tract, were only pulled down in the historical-preservation-challenged 1960s.

Another Italian grape grower in Burbank was the John Grangetto Winery on Scott Road. Like the others, it, too, was lost to the inexorable march of housing tracts.

## San Antonio Winery

Back in Los Angeles, another Italian family braved the growing Prohibition fervor and started the San Antonio Winery in 1917, on the east side of the river on lands once owned by Jean Louis Vignes. Those lands had become train yards by the time Santo Cambianica had arrived in town from northern Italy. Many of his countrymen worked in those yards, and from his small winery building, he began selling wine to them. A devout Catholic, he managed to get a contract from the archdiocese to provide altar wine all through the Prohibition period and beyond. The winery bought grapes from many sources, primarily the vineyards in Burbank, La Crescenta, Lamanda Park and San Gabriel. Cambianica and his nephew and the current head of the San Antonio Winery, Stephano Riboli, made home wine deliveries to their customers, which also helped the winery survive Prohibition and on into the explosive growth period of the city after World War II. Patiently, the winery expanded its operation and buildings in its largely industrial section of town, until today (at this writing) the winery is a big-scale, multifaceted operation known for its

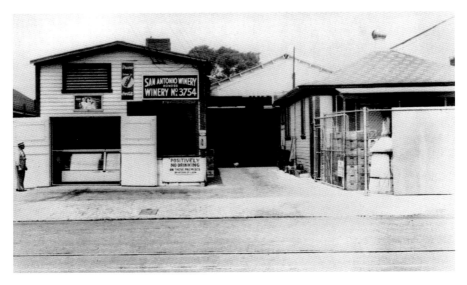

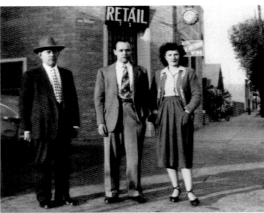

*Above*: Some of the original buildings of the San Antonio Winery in Lincoln Heights, (east) Los Angeles. The photo is most likely from the Prohibition era, with the (now) laughable sign out front prohibiting drinking. *Courtesy of the San Antonio Winery and Steve Riboli.*

*Left*: Founder Santo Cambianica (left) on the street in front of the winery, circa 1940s. With him is his nephew and his nephew's wife, Steve and Maddalena Riboli, the current owners. *Courtesy of the San Antonio Winery and Steve Riboli.*

wide selection of wines and hospitality. It has extensive vineyards in Paso Robles, Monterey County and the Napa Valley and even a winery annex just east of the old Guasti vineyards.

# CUCAMONGA

The large listing of Cucamonga Valley–area vineyards and wineries in the 1905 newspaper article included the Lafourcade brothers, John and August;

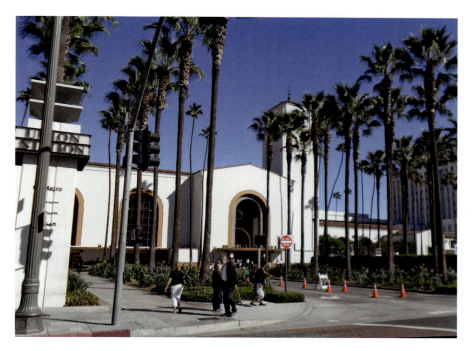

Union Station on Alameda Street in Los Angeles was once the location of Don Mateo Keller's vineyard and home that he built in the 1850s.

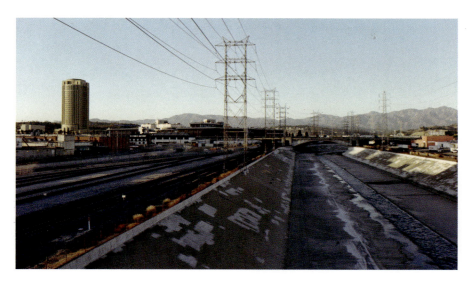

View from the First Street Bridge looking north over the Los Angeles River. This industrial area was once the vineyard of Jean Louis Vignes.

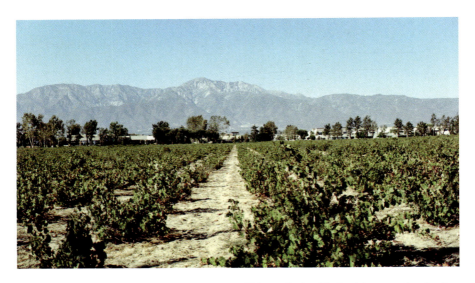

This vineyard in central Rancho Cucamonga still is producing Zinfandel grapes despite the encroaching urbanism.

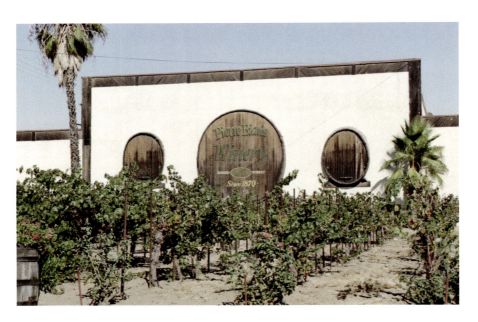

The Pierre Biane vineyard and winery in Rancho Cucamonga.

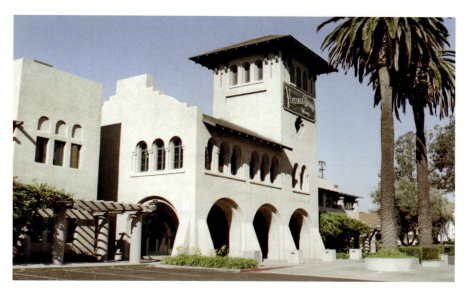

At Haven and Foothill in Rancho Cucamonga is the 1910 Mission Winery building and tower (later the Virginia Dare Winery), adaptively reused as offices.

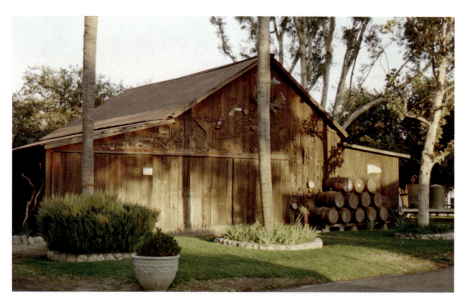

The old barn at the Galleano Winery displays a wide range of historic farming and vineyard equipment, set amid a visitors' information area.

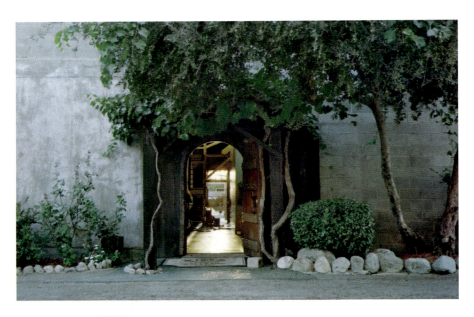

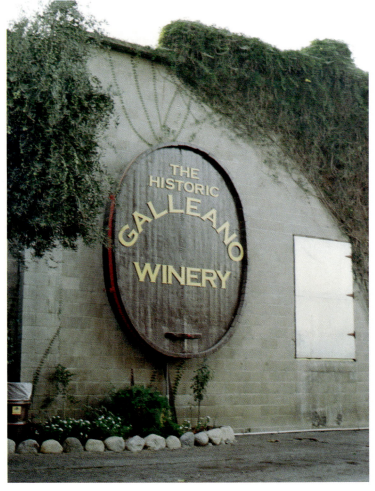

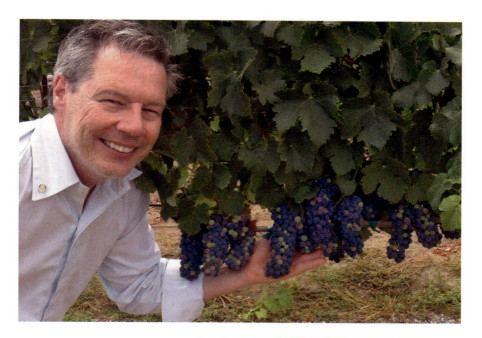

*Above*: Cucamonga Valley vintner Gino Filippi holds a cluster of Cabernet Sauvignon grapes in an Etiwanda vineyard. *Courtesy of Gino Filippi.*

*Right*: Gino Filippi (left), vintner at J. Filippi Winery in Rancho Cucamonga, and Don Galleano (right), vintner of the historic Galleano Winery in Mira Loma. *Courtesy of Gino Filippi.*

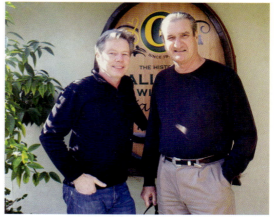

*Opposite, top*: The setting sun streams through the door to the Galleano Winery. Inside is one of the largest concrete fermentation tanks in the state.

*Opposite, bottom*: The entrance to the Galleano Winery. Don Galleano is the third-generation owner of this historic vineyard and winery that began operation in 1927.

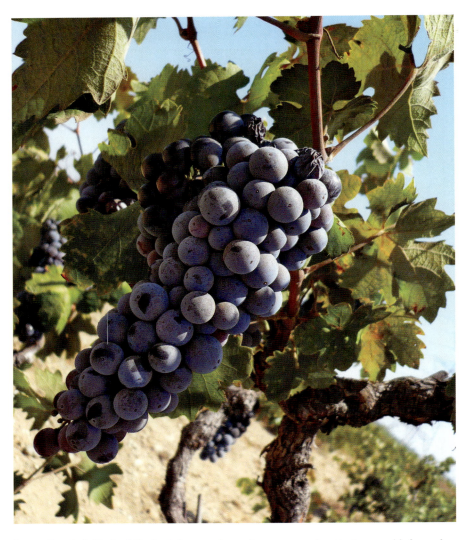

Lopez Ranch "old vine" Zinfandel grapes from vines over one hundred years old, farmed by Don Galleano. He sources them to other winemakers. *Courtesy of Gino Filippi and Steve Amoan.*

*Opposite, top*: The San Antonio Winery on Lamarr Street east in Lincoln Heights is the only winery left in the original vineyard areas of Los Angeles. *Courtesy San Antonio Winery.*

*Opposite, bottom*: The Barrel Room at the San Antonio Winery in Los Angeles. *Courtesy San Antonio Winery.*

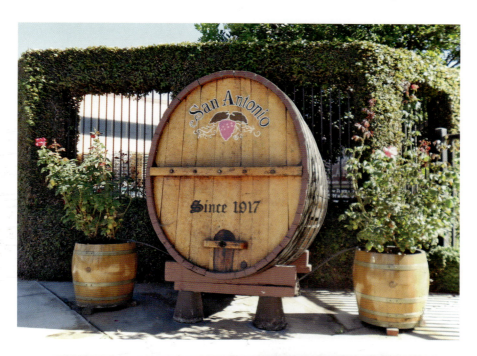
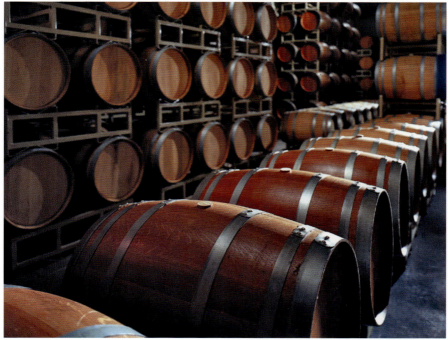

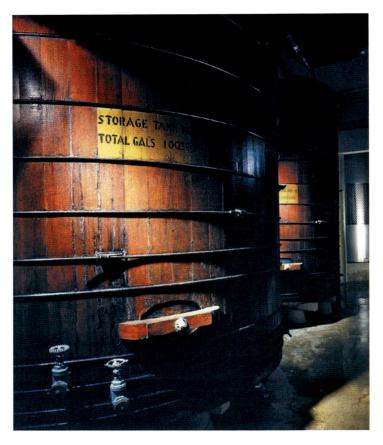

Ancient redwood storage tanks at San Antonio Winery in Los Angeles. *Courtesy San Antonio Winery.*

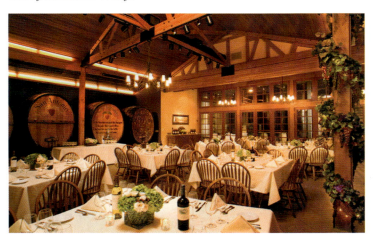

The main dining hall of Maddalena Restaurant at San Antonio Winery in Los Angeles. *Courtesy San Antonio Winery.*

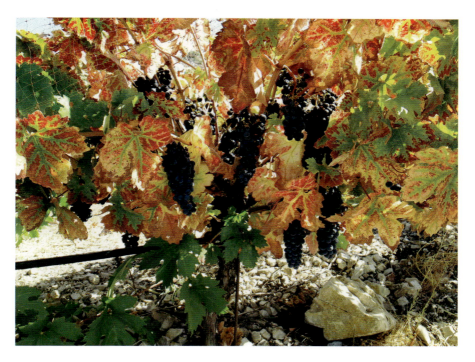

These Zinfandel grapes grown for San Antonio at Quarry Heights Vineyard in Paso Robles are ready for harvest. *Courtesy San Antonio Winery.*

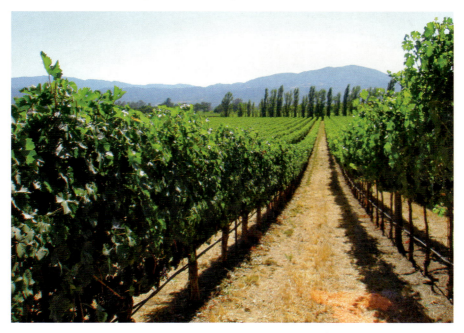

San Antonio Winery has a presence in the Napa Valley with this Riboli Rutherford Vineyard, named for the winery owners. *Courtesy of the winery.*

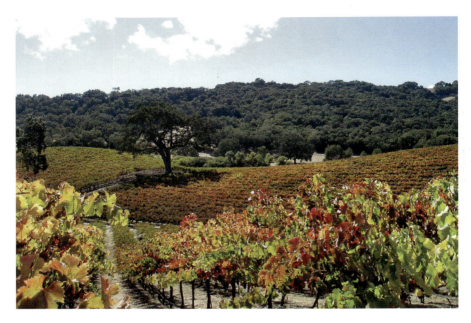

San Antonio's Pretty Penny Vineyard in Paso Robles at fall harvest time. *Courtesy of the winery.*

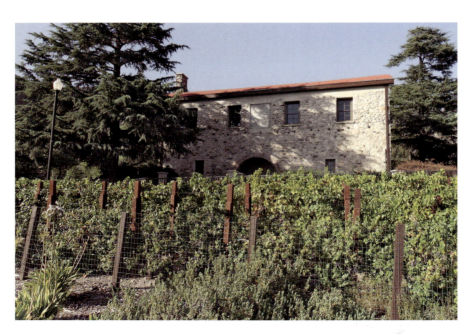

The old Le Mesnager stone barn and vineyard high on the slopes of the Deukmejian Wilderness Park in Glendale–La Crescenta.

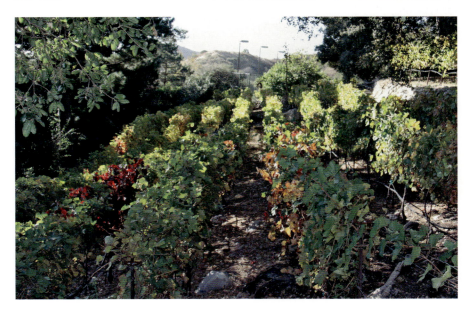

*Right*: A happy volunteer harvests the grapes in the Deukmejian Park vineyard above La Crescenta on a late afternoon in September.

*Below*: Beinn Bhreagh Vineyard at the McDonald family's home in La Crescenta. These Pinot Noir vines are grown at a high altitude (about 2,600 feet). *Courtesy of Tim McDonald.*

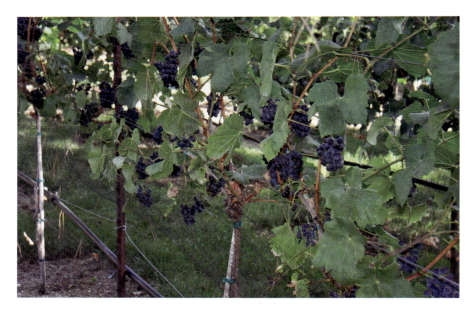

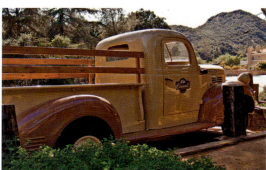

*Above*: Beinn Bhreagh Vineyard Pinot Noir grapes near harvest time. *Courtesy of Tim McDonald.*

*Left*: An old ranch truck at the Cornell Winery in Agoura. Cornell is emblematic of the recent surge of vineyards and wineries. *Courtesy of Bill Jones.*

*Opposite, top*: Like a castle/palazzo in Tuscany, this wine estate in Malibu rides its magnificent hilltop site, surrounded by vineyards climbing the steep slopes.

*Opposite, middle*: This vineyard and home in Malibu's Decker is sited at a high elevation. It's a scene reminiscent of the mountainous regions of Provence in France.

*Opposite, bottom*: These golden poppies growing among the vines identify Colcanyon Estate as being in California, rather than France. *Courtesy of John Freeman.*

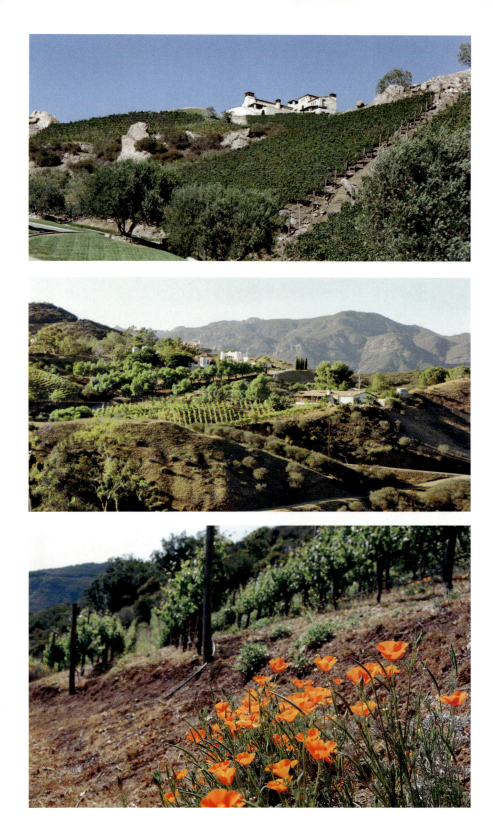

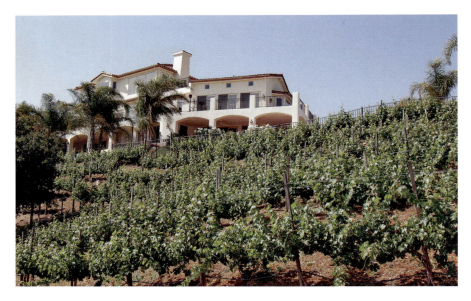

Vines on the steep hillsides of Colcanyon Estate Wines in Malibu, with the home and winery buildings on the ridge top above. *Courtesy of John Freeman.*

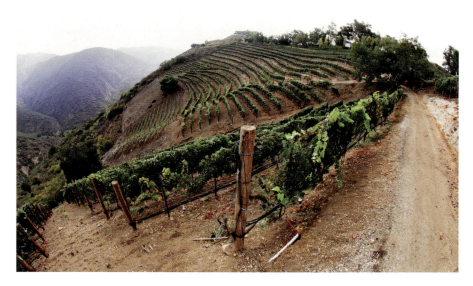

The vertiginous topography in the canyons of the Santa Monica Mountains will always circumscribe vineyard operations, despite the dramatic and inspiring vistas to be had. *Courtesy of Jessica and Gary Peterson, Trancas Vineyards.*

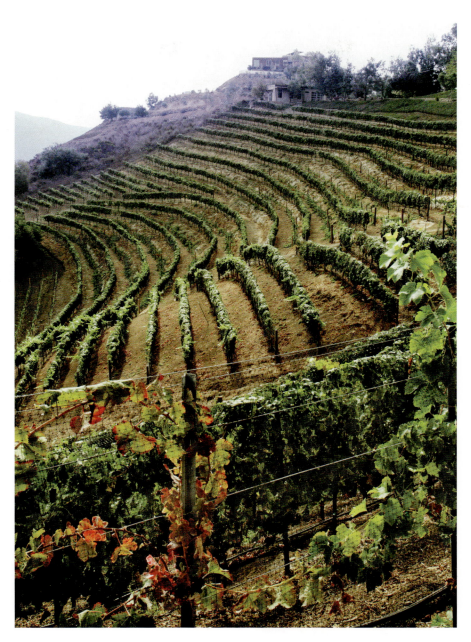

Vines on the steep hillsides in the canyons of Malibu, with the winery buildings on the ridge top, a common occurrence in this challenging topography. *Courtesy of Jessica and Gary Peterson, Trancas Vineyards.*

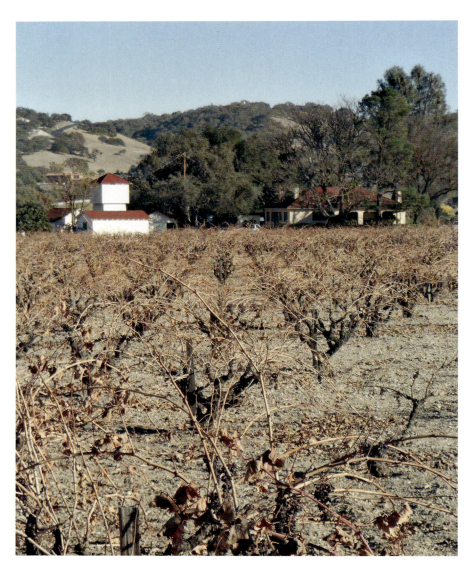

This present-day vineyard in Paso Robles could have easily stepped out of a nineteenth-century view of the Los Angeles countryside.

# A History from the Mission Era to the Present

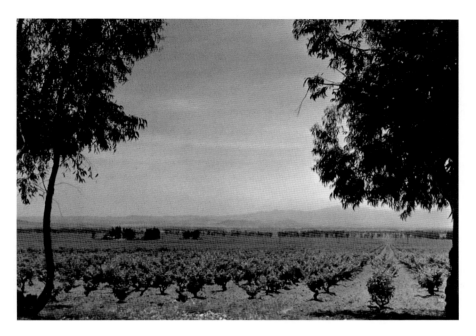

A Cucamonga Valley vineyard in an undated view. *Courtesy of Los Angeles Public Library Photo Collection.*

Cucamonga Winery Co.; the huge Italian Vineyard Co., which had an office in Los Angeles and still owned the West Glendale Winery; E. Vache & Co. in Brookside; Jacques Tisnerat and Pierre Espiau in Pomona; Sandoz & Guichou in Chino; and John Kaus in San Bernardino.

## Guasti

In 1900, Secundo Guasti founded one of the most significant winery and vineyard operations in Southern California: the Italian Vineyard Company. It effectively moved the center of gravity of vineyards and winemaking out of the traditional areas of Los Angeles and the San Gabriel Valley and into the Cucamonga Valley. Its huge acreage of vineyards—over five thousand acres—provided that influence, and it billed itself as the "largest winery in the world."

An immigrant from Asti, in the Piedmont region of northern Italy, Guasti arrived in Los Angeles in 1878. He ran the Hotel Italia Unita on Olvera Street for a time and very likely worked for the Pelanconi Winery

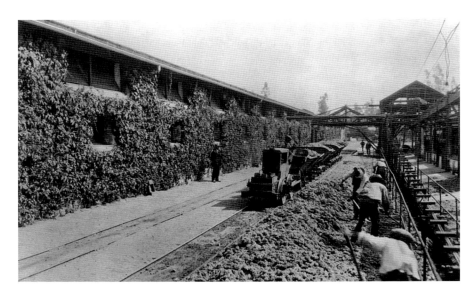

The famous grape-harvesting railroad operation at the Italian Vineyard Co. and winery in Guasti, east of Pomona, at the turn of the last century. *Courtesy of Cal Poly Pomona Library Special Collections.*

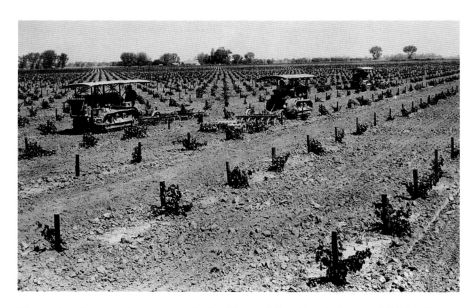

Vineyard maintenance by tractor at Italian Vineyard Co., Guasti. *Courtesy of Cal Poly Pomona Library Special Collections.*

# A History from the Mission Era to the Present

and vineyards. Guasti started his first winery, the West Glendale Winery, in 1894, located on San Fernando Road and Milford Street. Just north of his vineyard, across Verdugo Creek and its intersection with the Los Angeles River, were the Pelanconi vineyards. The current neighborhood where Guasti's winery stood is appropriately called Vineyard. A full-page ad in the 1895 Pasadena City Directory invites interested parties to visit the winery on San Fernando or its office and wine vault on Alameda at the corner of Third Street in Los Angeles.

Visiting the Cucamonga Valley east of Pomona, Guasti realized that the water runoff from the mountains continued under what appeared to be a sand desert but would be a fine place for grape growing without irrigation. In an era when the scourge of phylloxera devastated vineyards in the north of the state, the deep, sandy soil appeared to make vines immune to the disease. That recognition prompted even more planting. He sold shares to finance the vineyard, in the manner of an agricultural co-op or colony along the lines of Sbarboro's Italian Swiss Colony in northern California. He built houses for the workers, a stone church in the eighteenth-century style of

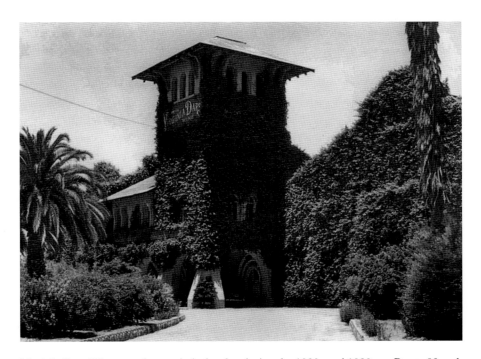

Virginia Dare Winery and tower in its heyday during the 1920s and 1930s on Route 66 and Haven Avenue in Cucamonga. *Courtesy of Cal Poly Pomona Library Special Collections.*

one in his hometown and more community buildings. The massive stone cellars for fermentation and aging were begun in 1904, built with the native stone from the river courses coming out of the mountains. It ultimately had a capacity of five million gallons. Very shortly, he had hundreds of his countrymen working for him. The Accomazzo family came with him from the West Glendale Winery and later went on to open their own winery in Cucamonga. Guasti persuaded his winemaking mentor, Claudio Ellena, to come out from Asti and work for him. Much later, the Ellena brothers had their own winery and brand: Regina. In this way, Guasti introduced a distinct Italian component to the Cucamonga winemakers that is still present today. Secundo Guasti died in 1927, and his son followed in 1933. The Italian Vineyard Company went into other hands. The stone winery buildings remain today, but they are silent and empty. The little stone church remains as well, but it still serves as a parish church.

## Mission Winery

In 1910, John Klusman and C.W. Post founded the Mission Winery. It had one thousand acres of vines and a capacity of 1.5 million gallons of wine. It is no coincidence that the winery buildings were designed in the then-popular Mission style. With their muscular buttresses, rough "shot-crete" surfaces and curving roof edges, the buildings make a strong statement. The tower that rises above the rest—and pulls the entire ensemble together—is one of the most evocative and romantic pieces of this architectural genre in Southern California. John Klusman was a German immigrant, arriving in 1894. He worked in several Cucamonga wineries before building the winery with his partner. When Prohibition was established in San Bernardino County in 1916, it caused Brookside Winery to cease operation. Klusman persuaded its now out-of-work owner, Marius Biane, to run the Mission Winery and vineyard. Only a few years later, Klusman and Post sold out to the Garrett Companies, one of the largest winemaking and marketing organizations in the country. Winemaker Biane went with the sale. Mission Winery was perfectly positioned (with its large capacity) to be Garrett's flagship enterprise in Southern California, selling its most popular wine, Virginia Dare. It reflected Paul Garrett's Virginia roots and sense of history. The sign with that name is still on the tower of the repurposed winery buildings, still at the corner of Haven and Foothill Boulevards in Rancho Cucamonga.

## Prohibition

As the likely passage of the Prohibition amendment moved closer, wineries and retail stores began to unload their stock or put it in storage. The Eighteenth Amendment passed the Nebraska legislature on January 16, 1919, meaning it would go into effect one year later. The actual enabling legislation—the Volstead Act—was passed by Congress on October 28, 1919. The general populace began to realize the enormity of the situation, causing a last-

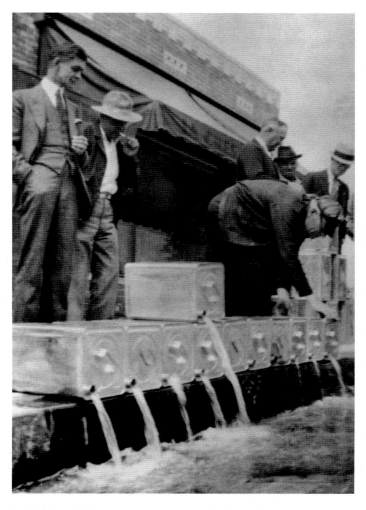

Prohibition raid in Montrose, circa 1920s. *Courtesy Glendale Public Library.*

minute rush on all forms of alcohol. Prices shot up in the last days before the law went into effect in January 1920. Most wineries then closed down, even as they struggled to find alternative uses for their product. But it seemed to be the end of the line for the wine business in the United States.

A few wineries were able to stay open by using one of the law's exemptions for sacramental or altar wine. Some wine was allowed for medicinal purposes. What medical problems were solved by wine were gray areas, and further legislation dealt with this loophole. But these wineries were licensed by the Bureau of Prohibition (part of the Treasury Department) and closely watched. San Antonio Winery was able to stay in business because of its wine contract with the Catholic Archdiocese of Los Angeles. The Italian Vineyard Company in Guasti did the same.

Inevitably, certain wineries still maintained an illegal business supplying restaurants, social clubs and the like. But who was supplying what to whom was never really known; to get into the record books, one had to be arrested. At the beginning, the Prohibition police were relentless; at its end, only the most egregious were prosecuted.

One exemption in the law brought a surprising response (at least to the makers of the law). It allowed each head of household to make up to two hundred gallons of "fruit juices" for his family's personal consumption. Once this aspect of the Volstead Act became well known, the increase in home winemaking for "personal consumption" skyrocketed throughout the country. It seemed no one saw this coming. But it was an unexpected boon for vineyard owners (though not for wineries), and they quickly moved on the opportunity. In 1920, there were about 300,000 acres of bearing vineyards in California. At the height of the boom in 1927, acreage was approaching 577,000. Grape production doubled from 1920, 1.25 million tons, to 1927, 2.5 million. Prices went from twenty-five dollars a ton to two or three times that. Vineyard property followed suit.

The primary transport of wine grapes from California to the East Coast cities were the railroads. They, too, rushed to serve this exploding business. In 1920, more than twenty-six thousand rail cars of grapes went east out of California; in 1927, it went past seventy-two thousand. In the first full year of Prohibition, the Sierra Madre Vintage Co. of Lamanda Park alone shipped sixty boxcars loaded with grape boxes to clients in Pittsburgh and Philadelphia. It did a similar amount of shipping every year after, until the vintage company closed in the late 1920s.

Vine growers now began to pull up their grape varieties that were incapable of withstanding the long shipment to the east. They began planting tougher,

# A History from the Mission Era to the Present

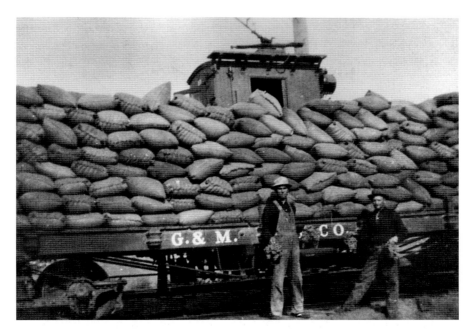

Workers holding grape bunches in front of grape sack–loaded flatcar from the Glendale and Montrose Railway, circa 1920s. *Courtesy Glendale Public Library.*

high-producing grapes that would arrive fresh and unbruised and look good. Table and raisin grapes were also added to this mix to be sent east. One particular variety that found widespread favor among growers was Alicante Bouschet. It was tough, a high producer and—unlike so many other red varieties—has a rich, ruby-red color at crushing, guaranteed to sell and look magnificent. The demand by home winemakers was almost entirely for red grapes, with the resulting drastic decline in white grape plantings. Many growers began adding (supposed) warning labels in the boxes to the effect of: do not add yeast, or fermentation will occur.

Fresh grapes shipped to home winemakers had always been part of the business of California vineyards, despite its huge rise at the beginning of Prohibition. This was directly attributable to the large increase of immigration to the United States of people from the Mediterranean area and southeastern Europe. Their ancient culture—formed by the Mediterranean agricultural trinity of grapes, olives and wheat—took for granted wine as a daily beverage. Italians were the largest portion of this immigrant grouping and the largest home winemakers. Police in these communities often quipped that they could tell when the grape trains had arrived because the neighborhoods smelled like wineries. So it was in those immigrant communities in Los Angeles. Italians, Mexicans, Croatians, Serbs, Greeks and Spaniards all crowded together in the older sections of downtown Los Angeles, Chinatown and Boyle Heights ("Bo-lights," to the Croatians). Quite often, they had large (always basement) winemaking operations that—of course—greatly exceeded the two-hundred-gallon maximum. Because they were immigrants with a winemaking heritage, the prohibition against it just made no sense. They were also vulnerable to language and cultural misunderstandings with the natives; many a basement wine cellar was "raided" and the barrels broken open or carried off.

Because fresh grape shipping had all the effects of an economic boom, it soon had its own crash. By 1926, overproduction had been reached, and prices began to drop. Growers were now in the same bind (largely of their own making) as wineries had been in 1920. They began to band together in co-ops or sell out to larger entities, struggling to find a way to survive. The largest co-op was Fruit Industries, which organized to take advantage of the price stabilization measures of the Federal Farm Board in 1929. The chairman of the board was Paul Garrett, whose roots were in eastern vineyards but who owned considerable California properties, most notably his large Virginia Dare winery and vineyard in Cucamonga. He boldly proposed a compromise product to the Prohibition Board that would be approved and still within the law. The wine-like product the company created was Vine-Glo, which sold well—so much so, the news reporting said, that Al Capone banned it from Chicago under pain of death. Fruit Industries responded that it was not going to be intimidated by racketeers but would follow the law. The entire story turned out to be a marketing ploy. Such were the gyrations that were necessary by vineyard owners just to sell the product.

As Prohibition wore on, the population's attitude toward it began to change. It was increasingly clear that most people were just ignoring the law; it was simply unable to be enforced. People could see that it brought more crime, more vice and more disrespect for the legal system and made most people into hypocrites. In a desperate attempt to shore up Prohibition, more draconian measures were added to the existing laws. But it served to add further frustration to the populace and advertise the essential bankruptcy of the whole law itself.

Nevertheless, enforcement attempts continued. One of the biggest hauls of the Federal Prohibition police in Southern California was the raid on Baumgarteker's Winery at 278 North Avenue 19 in the Lincoln Heights section of Los Angeles. Early on a January morning in 1930, the Feds moved in and confiscated 700,000 gallons of wine and 200,000 gallons of brandy. They arrested five workers but not Mr. Baumgarteker. He had disappeared at the end of November 1929 and was never seen again. Frank Baumgarteker was a wealthy Los Angeles businessman, who had originally emigrated from Austria. It was rumored that he had been murdered by elements of the Chicago mob because he would not sell his Cucamonga vineyard to them.

By 1932, repeal of the Eighteenth Amendment seemed a distinct possibility. Prohibition supporters had lost their main base when the large Women's Organization came out in favor of repeal, with the Democratic party in the same camp. Repeal was also equated with new jobs that would alleviate the increasing unemployment of the Depression era caused by the stock market crash of 1929. Franklin D. Roosevelt's overwhelming victory in November cleared the way. In February 1933, a resolution for repeal passed the Senate and the House and went to specially elected conventions in each state (not the legislatures) for ratification. Their votes were already known, and on December 5, 1933—with the last state ratifying the Twenty-first Amendment—Prohibition ended.

*Chapter 10*

# FROM REPEAL TO THE PRESENT

E uphoria enveloped the wine business with the coming of repeal. Old wineries reopened and dusted off their rusting equipment. A multitude of new wineries were established. Everyone looked forward to a brighter day, anticipating a wave of pent-up demand for wine. But it did not happen.

Thomas Pinney points out the multifaceted problems that the resurgent wineries and vineyards faced as they attempted to undo the damage done by Prohibition. It took many frustrating years, with some of the obstructions still extant eighty years on. The Twenty-first Amendment was hardly a blanket repeal. It reads as more of a grudging acceptance and gives each state the right to regulate alcoholic beverages as it sees fit. The resultant balkanization of contradictory and confusing sets of regulations has hampered the business ever since. Don Galleano, of the historic Galleano Vineyard in Mira Loma, explained, "It's easier for me to sell wine to China than it is to Pennsylvania." Prohibition forces and attitudes were still strong, and the enabling legislation was more intent on controlling and taxing alcohol. Legislators feared that criminals would still take over alcohol-producing operations; governments at all levels needed new sources of revenue. Wine was still being classed with "Demon Rum" as something that was morally repugnant, not as a food for daily life. The non-taxed, pre-Prohibition days of the wine business were gone.

Reopened wineries were in shambles, with rotten barrels, rusted equipment and collapsing buildings—all things that would require a sizable investment and steady income stream, something very dicey in the Depression era. New wineries suffered from ignorance of basic winemaking techniques (such as simple sanitizing of barrels and equipment), with knowledgeable winemakers hard to come by, as they had retired or were out of the business.

Home winemakers continued on, taking with them a sizable portion of the market. Only fortified wines offered a way for wineries, considering the difficulty of making it at home. For years after, fortified wines and sweet wines dominated sales, especially in Southern California. But it is to the credit of the home winemakers (especially those of Mediterranean origin) that the idea of wine as a daily beverage was kept alive, with its concomitant connection to wine as an integral part of life and civilization.

Vineyards had their own problems: too many grapes and too many of the wrong kind for making a finer wine. Eating grapes and raisin grapes were the dominant vines, with the much maligned Alicante Bouschet as the principal red grape. Zinfandel was next, along with carignane—all three good grapes if planted in the right area. Cabernet, merlot and pinot noir grapes had been systematically pulled out in favor of those shipping grapes and were now so rare as to be nonexistent. White varieties were scarce. In the depressed economy, vineyardists resisted any large-scale change that would cost them what little profit they could wring out of what they had. The new research coming out of the University of California was listened to but not followed as a whole.

University and government research programs reconstituted themselves and quickly came up with innovative analyses of winemaking and viticulture. But it would take time for their suggestions and writings to break through what was an essentially conservative mindset in the wineries and vineyards.

By the end of the 1930s, many of the new and old wineries had gone out of business because of financial concerns.

The main overriding focus for the future of the wine business was wine quality. This would shape its evolution over the next forty-plus years: what is it, who defines it and how is it defined? The gradual shift in marketplace desires, marketing ideas, visionary (or just plain stubborn or maniacal) winemakers, the technical innovations of the universities (particularly UC–Davis) and banking support all brought about a new winemaking ethic in the 1960s and '70s. The old methods were reshaped and repurposed.

## Los Angeles and the Valleys

Giovanni Piuma reopened his winery and grocery store on Main Street near the old Plaza, as did Santa Fe Wines and many others. Piuma's son continued the store and winery into the late 1960s, when the building was torn down for a parking lot. Piuma Road in Malibu is named for him. San Antonio Winery continued to expand. The West Glendale Winery and vineyards started by Secundo Guasti succumbed to residential and commercial development. The large Pelanconi vineyards just up San Fernando Road near the border with Burbank were coming under considerable pressure to be subdivided for homes; by the end of World War II, it had happened.

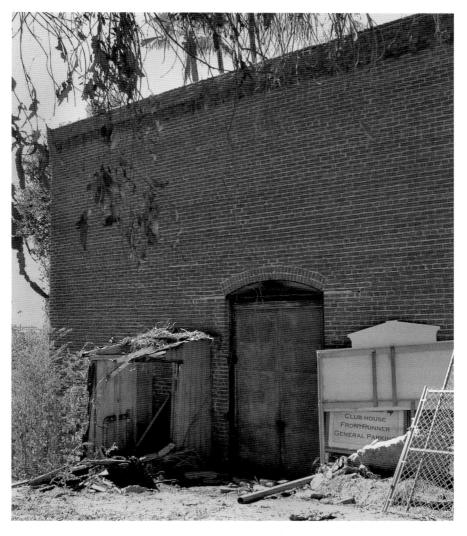

The east end of Baldwin's winery building of the 1870s. *Author's collection, courtesy of Santa Anita Racetrack.*

The Burbank wineries lasted longer. The large winery of John McClure on the slopes of the Verdugos was subdivided in the early '50s. Grangetto lasted into the early 1960s, with the Brusso winery putting up the last resistance to the onslaught of housing developments and pressure from nearby Lockheed. The Brusso family closed their operation in 1967, when the old winery building was sitting in a sea of new houses. But its wine is still remembered: the founder of Patagonia clothing recalled growing up in that part of the valley, and sneaking over to sample some of "Mama Brusso's jug wine."

Though the wineries of Lamanda Park had shut down in the 1920s and '30s (Pasadena had been a resolutely "dry" city), the vineyards remained untended (at least commercially). Hastings Ranch was taken over by the military in World War II, with much of its training maneuvers taking place among the old vines. Lamanda Park was annexed by the city of Pasadena, and housing subdivisions covered the vineyard areas where the Craig and Hastings Ranches had been. Kinneloa Mesa housing tract on the slopes above Eaton Canyon memorializes the ranch and vineyard of Abbott Kinney, who also developed the seaside community of Venice Beach. Sierra Madre Vintage Company is now remembered only by the names of certain streets in the vicinity of its winery buildings that were headquartered on Foothill Boulevard at Vinedo (Spanish for vineyard): Vineyard, Vine Alley, Del Vina, Mataro (evidence of some of the grape varieties grown) and, farther north, Brigden Road for its founder. Recently, Pasadena established Vina Vieja Park on the vanished vineyard property.

The only tangible remains of E.J. "Lucky" Baldwin's winemaking operation is his 1870s brick winery building, still in existence on the north side of the Santa Anita Racetrack. It retains its imposing sensibility but today is a storage facility.

## Crescenta Valley

Up in La Crescenta, Prohibition's end dismayed supporters but delighted most. As the law expired, one drinking establishment in Montrose received the first new liquor license in Los Angeles County the day after, probably for the reason that it had never stopped serving alcohol. Preparations had already been made for the end of the law. A group of World War II veterans had formed a consortium to make wine that would be ready at the end of Prohibition in December 1933. They had rented the stone barn and

# A History from the Mission Era to the Present

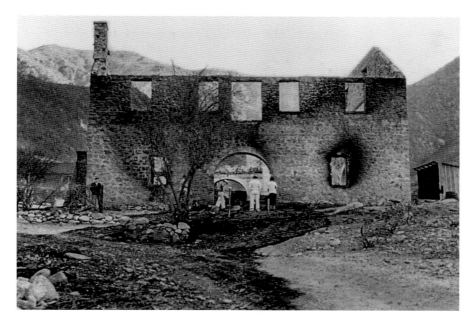

The Le Mesnager winery stone barn in Dunsmore Canyon, La Crescenta, burned out during the catastrophic November 1933 forest fire. The dark-stained earth in front is from thousands of gallons of wine that poured out from burning redwood and oak vats. *Courtesy Historical Society of the Crescenta Valley.*

winemaking equipment and harvested the grapes of the Le Mesnager family property in Dunsmore Canyon. Now that their harvest was finished and the wine was fermenting, all they had to do was bottle their crush at the appointed time. But disaster struck. In November, a forest fire consumed the front face of the San Gabriel Mountains in the Crescenta-Canada Valleys, burning down the wood roof and the inner wood frame of the stone barn; all the redwood vats and oak barrels containing the new wine of the veterans went up in flames. Over twenty thousand gallons of wine spilled out through the barn doors, staining the earth red.

But Mother Nature wasn't through. On January 1, 1934, after days of steady rain and a large downpour on New Year's Eve, a huge flood burst out from all the canyons that had been denuded by the fire, devastating the valley below. Giant boulders larger than two cars landed on Foothill Boulevard after tearing through homes and buildings; the wall of debris (including mud, rocks and trees) mowed down everything in its path. Over twenty-eight people died, including the twelve who had reached the supposed safety of the American Legion Hall on Rosemont Street. The wall of water tore out

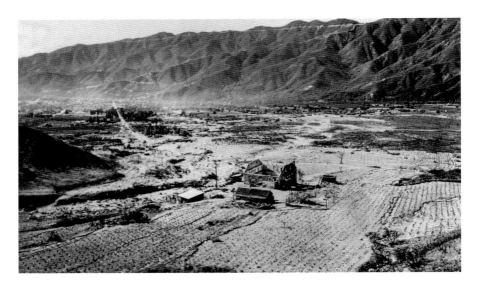

The burned-out and flood-ravaged Le Mesnager winery and vineyards, looking south to the Verdugo Mountains in January 1934. *Courtesy Glendale Public Library.*

a rear corner of the building, swirled the occupants around and then dragged them under as the torrent continued down the slope into Verdugo Canyon. The Le Mesnager vineyard was buried under a layer of debris, with just a little of each vine protruding through. Similar events happened in other vineyards in the valley that were in the path of the debris flows. One would think that the spirit of Prohibition was not about to give up, even in its last gasp.

The Le Mesnager family rebuilt the stone barn with a barrel vault roof in place of the original gable-ended roof that had had three dormer windows on each side. The new interior had a second-floor mezzanine for living, complete with two fireplaces, and the family moved in. They continued to work the vineyard, making wine and brandy. World War II slowed the operation, and it was only fitfully used thereafter. The postwar population boom in Southern California also came to the Crescenta Valley. The family's Le Mesnager Land and Water Company was more valuable than their vineyards; it had been the main source of their income from the 1920s through the 1950s. Some of the company's waterworks (wells, piping and a stone cistern clinging to a hillside) can still be seen in Dunsmore and Cook Canyons. Louis Sr.—who was the real builder of the stone barn—died in 1957, and his son, Louis Jr. (Louie), continued to live there with his family until the seven-hundred-plus-acre ranch was sold to a housing developer in the late 1960s.

# A History from the Mission Era to the Present

Almost immediately, opposition to the proposed housing gained steam, particularly from the neighborhood directly below. As elsewhere in the built-out, suburbanized (and now crowded) Southland, La Crescenta in the 1970s did not have the same issues as those of the 1940s. The city of Glendale had annexed a swath of the Crescenta Valley in 1952 that included the Le Mesnager properties in Dunsmore and Cook Canyons. Delays and legal wrangling between the city and the developer continued into the 1980s, until the city proposed a buyout of the developer in 1984. The city had plans for a wilderness-style park that would preserve the property. The money was cobbled together from a cash-strapped Glendale and donations from the Santa Monica Mountains Conservancy. The then governor of California—George Deukmejian—added the last millions, and the land was purchased in 1989. Because of his personal efforts to secure the last bit of funding, the park is named in his honor: Deukmejian Wilderness Park.

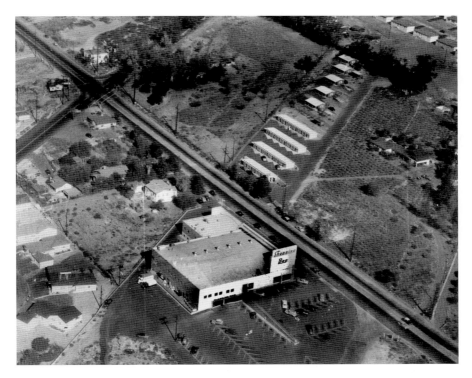

An aerial view of the Shopping Bag market on Foothill Boulevard in La Crescenta in the 1940s. This was a typical Southern California pattern of urban development encroaching on—and eventually covering—flourishing vineyard land. *Courtesy Glendale Public Library.*

Elsewhere, vineyard land was not so fortunate in being saved for reuse. From Sunland-Tujunga through La Canada, the story was the same: exuberant resurgence after Prohibition, recognition that it was still the Depression, followed by World War II constraints and then a postwar housing boom that ripped out the vines. Some vineyards made a go of it; the Fitzgerald property in the Seven Hills area of Tujunga, and the Petrottas' in La Canada lasted longer than others. The large Kirst family vineyards of La Canada above Foothill Boulevard, bordering the Arroyo Seco, began to be developed into a housing tract in 1945. It was the setting of Bailey Park in the celebrated movie *It's a Wonderful Life*. The elegant Kirst mansion and remaining ranch buildings were taken by the Foothill Freeway in the mid-1960s. By the early '70s, all the old vineyards had been pulled out for housing developments. The Hall Ranch above Alta Canyada still has its old winery barn on a sizeable piece of property, but no vineyards are to be seen on the land.

## Cucamonga

On the day of repeal, the Cucamonga Valley Winery sent a case of wine to President Roosevelt as a gesture of thanks. As the largest contiguous area of vineyards and wineries in the Southland, these Cucamonga businesses had survived and thrived in Prohibition. In 1934, there were over twenty-seven thousand acres in vines that covered the area between the Los Angeles, San Bernardino and Riverside Counties. Over the next twenty years, it was the fastest-growing wine region in the country. By the late 1940s, that twenty-seven thousand acres had grown to over forty-five thousand, with approximately sixty wineries. The valley's acreage was more than in the Napa Valley. But the growing size and power of the Central Valley overshadowed all other areas in vine acreage and wine production gallonage. Part of this massive, post-Prohibition expansion was the Galleano Winery, established as a commercial business in 1933, out of the Galleano family's purchase of the historic Cantu ranch and vineyard in 1927. Arriving in the United States in 1913 from their native northern Piemonte, Italy, Domenico and Lucia Galleano joined their elder brothers, Angelo and John, in a dry-farming operation in Huntington Park, California. They worked in other vineyards until Domenico and Lucia bought the Cantu property and ranch buildings. Through succeeding generations, the winery has become one of the largest,

## A History from the Mission Era to the Present

still-extant winemaking operations in the Cucamonga area, with planted varieties typical of the valley: Zinfandel, Grenache, Mourvedre, Muscat of Alexandria, Burger and the local Mission.

However, the Cucamonga Valley vintners and growers were the heirs of the wine heritage of Los Angeles, even as that city surpassed San Francisco in population, leaving no room for agriculture, let alone vineyards. Despite Los Angeles' growth, its county was the number-one agricultural county in the nation as late as the 1940s. Its county fair at Pomona was important for many farm products; local wineries submitted their wine for the annual wine tasting awards, where the Cucamonga wineries were always present. But in the aftermath of Prohibition, they, too, were embroiled in those struggles that afflicted other vineyards and wineries in California.

With the end of World War II shortages and restraints, the old Italian Vineyard Co. winery and 5,000 acres of vines was sold by H.O. Lanza to Garrett and Co. in one of the biggest deals of 1945. Other expansion occurred as Vai Brothers (Padre Winery) bought 1,300 acres of vineyard in Mira Loma in 1946. The town used to be known as Wineville. It changed its name in 1930 to its current one, some said, because it sounded too "wet" for the dry times of Prohibition. Actually, it was to get out of the shadow of a gruesome murder that occurred there, sensationalized throughout the Southland and chronicled in the 2012 movie *The Changeling*. In 1939, there were forty-one bonded wineries, with a fermentation capacity of thirteen million gallons. By the mid-1940s, this had grown to fifty-five wineries, with 35,000 acres of vines.

One of the largest operations was Brookside Winery. From 1952 to 1973, Marius Biane (pronounced like "beyond," minus the *D*), with his sons Philo and Francoise, expanded into the old winery building of the Italian Vineyard Co. and created retail stores (mini-wineries) all over the state to sell their wine direct from the winery. When Philo retired in 1973 (after Brookside was bought by Beatrice Foods), he created his own award-winning sherry winery: Rancho de Philo. With his daughter currently running the winery, the Vache Freres family winemaking tradition has been brought into the twenty-first century.

In the 1970s, winemakers like the Opici Winery (now the location of Vineyard Junior High School), Thomas Brothers, Cucamonga Vineyard Co., the Aggazzotti family, Cherpin Brothers, Galleano Winery and J Filippi Vintage Co. (including the large, solely vineyard operations of the Hofer family and the de Ambrogio family) were dealing with market forces and changing tastes in wine. Cucamonga still made over 90 percent of the wine in the southern wine district (the six southern counties), even as urbanization

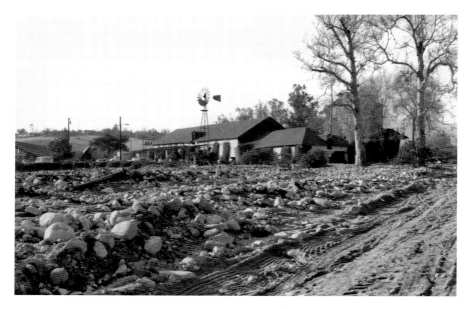

The historic Thomas Winery in Rancho Cucamonga. On January 25, 1969, after days of torrential rains, a wall of debris from the nearby raging creek crashed over the old winery (at the time owned by the J. Filippi family of winemakers). Priceless antiques and historic artifacts from winemaking were destroyed. A portion of the original 1839 Tapia homestead was washed away. A month later, a second flood continued the destruction. *Courtesy of Gino Filippi, J. Filippi Winery.*

began to cover over the prime growing areas. Smog, blown in from Los Angeles, was a major concern degrading vine growth. Brookside Winery began planting new vineyards in the Temecula Valley, south of Riverside in 1967, followed by Eli Callaway, which began a revitalized wine outlook for Southern California.

Nationally, winemakers were finally able to establish certain quality and labeling requirements with the creation of a system of American Viticulture Areas (AVA) since 1978 to define wine growing regions. Wine using a geographic label indication had to signify the kind and amount of any certain grape on the label. It was a boon for all and a uniquely American version of the European *appellation controlee* or *denominacion de origin*. Symbolically, the Missouri area of Hermann was given AVA #1, in the spirit of George Husman, Eugene Hilgard and the other experimenting German viticulturalists of the nineteenth century. Cucamonga Valley received an AVA designation in 1995, largely through the efforts of Gino Filippi.

A History from the Mission Era to the Present

# Today

The resurgence of vineyards and winemaking in the Los Angeles area mirrors the explosion of wineries and vinelands throughout the state. Though not on the large scale of the past, here and there one can see winemaking operations that range from backyard, "shade-tree" fermenters to wineries of several acres in Los Angeles County. The Moraga Vineyards can be seen on the slope across the valley of the Sepulveda Pass as you take the tram to the Getty Center. The Malibu area has three of its own AVA designations, with some estimates of over fifty vineyards climbing up the steep hillsides. Vineyards are flourishing in the Antelope Valley/Agua Dulce areas. High up in the canyons of the San Gabriels, steep-sloped vineyards are being staked out. Even in older neighborhoods like Highland Park, Eagle Rock, Silverlake and Echo Park, small vineyards are being planted in any available open space.

However, there have been some setbacks recently. The Los Angeles County Board of Supervisors voted to prohibit any vineyards in the Santa Monica Mountains area, which includes the Malibu region. This action has essentially deprived these vineyard owners of their property and their hard work. Hopefully, the board will reconsider its action and rescind its unjust law.

In the Cucamonga AVA, there is a concerted effort to save and transplant threatened "old-vine" Zinfandel plants to interested parties. Many of these heritage Zinfandel and other varieties have already been moved on to the Cal Poly Pomona campus. According to special collection librarian Danette Cook Adamson of Cal Poly Pomona, "Don Galleano deserves credit for saving wine grape plants from the De Ambrogio vineyards in Rancho Cucamonga that are more than one hundred years old. Those plants live on here now at Cal Poly Pomona and are the source of our Horsehill Vineyards Zinfandel wine." The Galleano Winery farms many other acres of these old-vine, Zinfandel grapes, which are highly prized by other vintners up and down the state for their unique taste profile.

Several years ago, J. Filippi Winery (housed in the old Ellena Brothers/Regina Winery in Rancho Cucamonga) collaborated with noted enologist Denis Lurton from Bordeaux, France, to produce a highly sought-after cabernet blend, which they named Deux Mondes Reserve. The grapes were all a product of the Etiwanda area of the valley.

Rancho Cucamonga is particularly sensitive to its wine heritage. Many of the new buildings going up on old vineyard properties have deliberately planted "mini-vineyards" as part of their landscaping schemes. On Haven

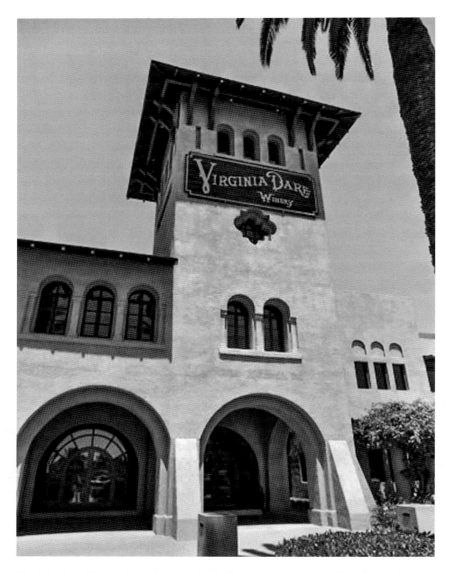

Virginia Dare Tower with palm tree, 2012. Compare this to the earlier picture from the 1920s. The tower and part of the winery buildings have been repurposed to its current form as office buildings at the corner of Haven and Foothill Boulevards in Rancho Cucamonga. *Author's photo.*

Avenue south of Foothill Boulevard, the vines are particularly noticeable. The city was instrumental in having portions of the old Mission/Virginia Dare Winery buildings—including the magnificent tower—saved and

## A History from the Mission Era to the Present

repurposed to its current commercial incarnation. The same was done for the old Thomas Winery—the original Cucamonga Winery of Tiburcio Tapia—in the shadow of the Red Hill site of Tapia's adobe. For over thirty years, residents have held a Grape Harvest Festival in town to celebrate that history. Despite not having a "vineyard preserve" overlay zone like that in the Napa Valley, the wine traditions and heritage are alive in this valley, which includes the Galleano Winery, the Fillipi Winery, the Rancho de Philo (Biane) Winery and an annex of the San Antonio Winery.

Other cities are quietly recognizing their own wine history in their own fashion. Burbank Historical Society has displays and artifacts from those wineries (Brusso, Gai, Grangetto and McClure) that once were prominent in the city up through the 1960s. Some of the docents are personally related to those earlier winemaking families and have their stories to tell. In Glendale, the city is in the process of restoring the great, two-story, stone barn of the Le Mesnager family at Deukmejian Wilderness Park. In a major remodel of the park in 2004–05, the city planted a small commemorative vineyard in front of the stone barn, in the very area where the vines of Old Hermitage Winery once grew. The city then asked the Historical Society of the Crescenta Valley to maintain the vineyard and provide programs on wine history of the area.

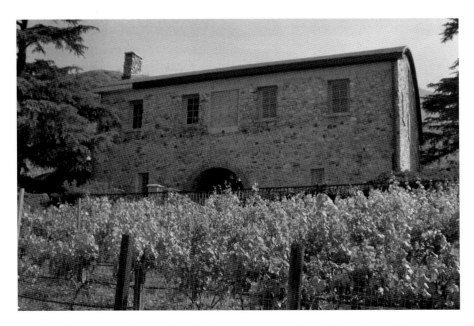

The Le Mesnager winery stone barn in its current restoration with the vineyard in Deukmejian Wilderness Park, Glendale–La Crescenta. *Author's collection.*

A sponsored organization of the society was formed in 2007 for that project, and now the Stone Barn Vineyard Conservancy is working on its seventh vintage, with more programs and tours being planned.

Perhaps other municipalities in the San Gabriel/San Fernando valleys—along with Los Angeles—will follow the examples of Rancho Cucamonga and Glendale and establish programs/vineyards (or physical displays) to celebrate and keep alive their own viticulture heritage, a heritage that was once so vital to the Los Angeles area that it defined the "Southern Vineyard" and has now become the iconic agriculture of California. Should more examples like that come to fruition, one can't help but think that old Jean Louis Vignes—Don Luis del Aliso—would be proud of the celebration of those achievements that he and his contemporaries started so long ago in the dusty little pueblo of Los Angeles beside the Rio Porciuncula.

*Appendix 1*

# WHERE WAS THE ORIGINAL "CASA" AND VINEYARD OF JOSE MARIA VERDUGO?

While researching the wine history of Los Angeles, this very provocative reference came up in Thomas Pinney's *History of Wine in America*: "Jose Maria Verdugo may have planted the first private, (non-mission) vineyard in California on his Rancho San Raphael." He had every opportunity to do so, based on his position as guardsman at the San Gabriel Mission, where the largest mission vineyard and winery of all was housed, and as possessor of one of the first cattle-grazing permits, given to him and two others (Dominguez and Nietos) at the same time in 1784. These permits were the precursors of the rancho land grants that were a major feature of the Spanish and Mexican periods of California.

Mission padres were perusing his land and others for a new mission site in 1795. Their journals mention the *"paraje de la zanja"* (the place of the water ditch) on the Rio Porciuncula (Los Angeles River) near Cahuenga Peak. While there, they also noted Verdugo's grain fields and another vegetable plot close by that was farmed by a "gentile" who also worked for Jose Maria. So in the ten years he had the property, he had improved it, despite the possibility of having it expropriated by the missionaries. (The improvements were actually done by his brother, Mariano de la Luz, as Jose Maria had to fulfill his duties at the mission.) That would seem to suggest that he might have planted his vineyard in the early to mid-1790s. His letter written to Governor Borica on December 4, 1797, petitioning for confirmation of his grant mentions his cattle, sheep and horses "as well as large crops." Eventually, the padres selected a site in the northern part of the valley, where Mission San Fernando

# Appendix 1

was established in 1798, the same year that the governor patented Verdugo's rancho. Later, an entry in the records of the Ayuntamiento (City Council) of Los Angeles on April 7, 1836, mentions the dam in the river at Cahuenga. Was it Jose Maria's or a later version?

So where was his vineyard? Was it close to his house? It must have been; vines and the harvest need that proximity for tending and winemaking. And where was his house? Jose Maria was fond of calling his rancho "La Zanja," rarely calling it Rancho San Raphael. If the padre's journals are correct, that would put the *zanja* near the great curve of the river, at the east end of the San Fernando Valley, where it turns south and enters the Narrows. It was the great collection spot for all the waters of the San Fernando Valley. In the Spanish period, the source of the river was considered to be a swampy area (*cienega*) below Cahuenga peak at the corner of Verdugo's rancho and the probable spot of his *zanja*.

The peculiar geology of the Los Angeles River in the Narrows involves a granite hardpan running under the river that rises higher than the adjacent areas out in the valley; it continues to where the river debouches out of the Narrows south of the old pueblo. The hard pan forces the south-flowing waters to the surface in this narrow stretch, giving the appearance of a larger, continuously flowing river. In the San Fernando Valley, it was more of a congeries of tributary rivulets; south of town, it often dissipated or disappeared altogether in the sands of the wide-open plains. This constancy of water would have been one of the reasons the Spanish located their second pueblo on this site; the easily watered, wide-open plains on three sides were perfect for the pueblo's agricultural needs.

Verdugo's rancho began at the northern pueblo limits, at a point where the Rio Porciuncula (Los Angeles River) and the Arroyo Hondo (Arroyo Seco) meet. The eastern boundary of the rancho followed the Arroyo all the way into the high mountains. The western limit was the Rio until just past the great curve. Then the line continued straight north to an area where La Tuna Canyon opens into the larger valley. The wheat fields that the padres alluded to were part of the requirement of a ranchero to provide a certain amount of *fanegas* (a Spanish unit of measure) of wheat for himself and the common weal. The other requirements were to build a house of stone corrals for horses and cattle and plant vineyards. A *zanja* to water these fields and a vineyard would not have been a huge undertaking on the Rio of that time. It didn't have the steep-walled, "concrete cliffs" (as some have called the concrete walls) of the river of today. Late nineteenth-century photos of the river show the water running in a somewhat wide and shallow swale,

# Appendix 1

its banks lined with willow trees; another shows a *zanja* with a weir near Griffith Park, which could easily have doubled for a similar one constructed by Verdugo with the materials and knowledge available at the time. The *zanja* would have led away eastward from the river to an area remote enough to be safe from a river in storm runoff. Jose Maria had experience of that at the first location of the San Gabriel mission. Sited at the Narrows (near Montebello and Pico Rivera) of the San Gabriel River, it had sustained considerable flood damage in a winter storm. After that, the padres moved it to its present location. He would have also prudently (let's at least give him credit for that) stayed away from Verdugo Creek and its confluence with the Rio just south of its curve. Just how destructive, capricious and widespread the river's path could be in storm time is echoed in a droll letter of a railroad engineer to the City Council of Los Angeles. After a particularly devastating flood in the 1880s, the engineer wrote that the railroad would be happy to build a new bridge over the Los Angeles River, if the council would but tell just where the river would be flowing and just how wide it would be.

In 1871, the Rancho La Zanja was broken up by the claims of various people. The "Great Partition" survey of the rancho of that year is a remarkable document in and of itself. Existing trails crisscrossing the rancho are shown, as are houses and ruins of houses. Very few house indications are shown on the eastern (Arroyo Seco) side of the rancho. Almost all house symbols are along Verdugo Road, south of where it leads out of Verdugo Canyon, or on the western stretch toward the Los Angeles River. Little field huts called "jackalls" (or the Spanish version, *jacales*) are quite literally strewn about the place. The Chaboya Tavern is shown near the river, along the road to San Fernando and the pueblo (about where today's Broadway crosses that road), with a multiplicity of trails leading to it. Chaboyas and Verdugos had intermarried. (Interesting to note that the current Golden Road Brewery and Pub are almost in the same spot as that Chaboya Tavern.)

At the curve of the river, on a rise just slightly to the east, and a stone's throw from the confluence of Verdugo Creek, is an indication of a house. Directly next to it is another house symbol labeled "ruin of Fernando Verdugo." Could that be it? Fernando was a later descendant of Jose Maria but alive as of the survey time period. It certainly would be in the vicinity of a *zanja* that was workable, even though there is no indication of a *zanja* anywhere on the survey. But would Jose Maria locate his house that close to the river, knowing its ferocity at flood stage? Perhaps it is a barn, a place to work his crops or perhaps his winemaking building. Through most of the nineteenth century, the area north and south of the confluence of Verdugo Creek and

# Appendix 1

the Los Angeles River and on the east side consisted of large vineyards. What is known now as the Pelanconi neighborhood was named for the early winemakers (Antonio and son Lorenzo) whose building still stands on Olvera Street in Los Angeles. South of the creek (in an area neighborhood now known as Vineyard) might have been vineyards from an early date, but the West Glendale Winery was there from 1894 on, started by Secundo Guasti, who later had the largest vineyard in the state (five thousand acres, circa 1910) east of Pomona. These two areas could very well have been Jose Maria's vineyard as well.

About a mile east, right on the north side of Verdugo Creek, is probably the most unique indication on the whole survey. It is a rectangle, several acres in extent, outlined with tree symbols and labeled "Old Orchard" (in the area of Central and Brand, Stocker and Glenoaks). No houses are shown in the immediate vicinity, but just due north and slightly west by many hundreds of feet is a double house indication with "ruin of Catalina Verdugo." Could that have been his original house? It is in the vicinity of the current Casa de Adobe on Dorothy Drive, though that house only started construction in 1871. Was there an original Jose Maria Verdugo house right there, remodeled or torn down during the present building's construction? Catalina was Verdugo's blind daughter. She had a house constructed for her by her brother Julio (most likely) in the years right after her father's death in 1831 in Verdugo Canyon. But she was heir to much of that western portion of the land in the Great Partition.

What was in the "old orchard"? Was it olives, oranges or vines? The San Fernando mission had two separate orchards, large in scale, where it grew all of those plants, surrounded by an adobe wall. An orchard of any size out on the flat plain would need some kind of protection from range animals, whether it was adobe or not. Trees planted close together, a hedge of nopales cacti (like that at mission San Gabriel) or willow tree stakes driven into the ground to provide a live fence (like that surrounding the vineyard plots at Anaheim) would do the job. Perhaps that was Jose Maria's original vineyard, augmented with other orchard plants. Would he have made a second *zanja* to irrigate this orchard with a weir in Verdugo Creek? Its watershed stretches up into La Crescenta and the mountains above, with the collected water of its year-round streams.

Perhaps the clinching evidence is the reminiscences of Jose Olivas, a resident of Glendale, who arrived in the vicinity in 1865. He was quoted in the *History of Glendale and Vicinity*:

# Appendix 1

*The oldest Verdugo house that I know of was the one near the corner of Pacific Avenue and Kenneth Road; the ruins were there not very long ago.* [Others say it was south of that intersection, more likely at Clement and Pacific, near Hoover High School, and a news article mentions that the ruins were still visible as late as 1915]...*there were three adobe houses along the foothills, west of the Thom property, the first was the Sepulveda place, used a few years ago as the "Casa Verdugo Restaurant"* [top of Brand Boulevard]; *then came the one built by Sheriff Sanchez* [the current Casa Adobe on Dorothy Drive], *and the third was the old Verdugo house* [the one he already mentioned]. *Then there was the one, still standing in Verdugo canyon* [Catalina's on Bonita Street], *and there was another in the canyon on the east side of the road just above the big Glendale reservoir. There was one over near Garvanza on top of a hill.* [Dora Verdugo remembers this place, saying it was near the Sparkletts Water Company.]

In support (to some degree) of Olivas's indication of the original casa are some other symbols on the 1871 survey. In that time period, surveyors would use small hatching marks to indicate vegetable gardens, field crops or vineyards of significant size. There are three large areas on the survey where the hatching occurs. One is in Verdugo Canyon on the flat lands in front of the Catalina Verdugo adobe, now traversed by Canada and Verdugo Boulevards. The second is on the lands that were deeded back to Julio Verdugo, roughly bounded by Verdugo on the east, Acacia on the south, Adams Street on the west and Colorado Street on the north. The largest of the three abuts the south slope of the Verdugo Mountains, Jackson Street or Louise Street to the west, Glenoaks Boulevard to the south and Rossmoyne on the east. However, none of these areas is labeled or has a legend to indicate what exactly is happening or growing there. We do know that of the 200 acres deeded back to Julio as part of the settlement, more than 120 acres were in vines below the hills, west of what became Verdugo Boulevard. Those vines were planted by Julio some years before. The hatching there (already mentioned) coincides with Julio's vineyard and would certainly be a clue as to the use of the two other areas. The largest area, abutting the Verdugo Mountains, has the same markings. Would this be the original vineyard? In his will of 1828, Jose Maria divides his rancho between his daughter Catalina and his only son, Julio, giving "the vineyard" (singular, not plural) to Catalina. If this is "the vineyard," it is close enough to her adobe in Verdugo Canyon to be in her sphere of influence. The

## Appendix 1

mountains close at hand would protect the vines (somewhat) and provide natural streams of irrigation from the canyons above. A *zanja* in the creek as it comes out of the canyon wouldn't be out of place.

A map of Glendale in 1936, drawn up as a popular, tourist-style map of important and historical places, shows an arrow pointing to the curve of the river as the site of Verdugo's *zanja* (where the ABC television studios are today). There is an indication of where the original house ruins are (at Clement and Pacific), verifying Olivas's memoir. Interestingly, the map also shows a long road paralleling Verdugo Creek on its north side, calling it "Camino Viejo" (author's quotes), portions of which are the current Monterey Road (appropriately), running west to cross the river somewhere in what is now Studio City and running east along the slopes of the hills past Verdugo Boulevard. It continues down along eastern Colorado Boulevard, skirting the southern hills as it makes the connection with Eagle Rock Boulevard into York Boulevard. It crosses the Arroyo Seco into South Pasadena, where it once again picks up the name of Monterey Road, continuing into what is now San Marino, where it ends at Huntington Drive, just north of mission San Gabriel. It is quite rightly called Camino Viejo (separate from the more famous Camino Real, yet a part of it), for it was the original road to Monterey that connected the missions of San Gabriel and San Buenaventura, long before mission San Fernando was founded.

The Verdugos seemed to have built several casitas all over their rancho for various members of their large family over the generations. In that, they were unlike many other rancheros who built just one large house that was added and remodeled to over the years, such as the Yorbas and the Lugos. The extant examples of these two-story buildings are the particularly fine Rancho Los Cerritos near Long Beach and the grand hacienda of General Mariano Vallejo at Rancho Petaluma in Sonoma County. Besides the two remaining Verdugo adobes, Julio Verdugo—Jose Maria's only son—built a home on his portion of the rancho in 1860, going into debt to do so, which caused the "Great Partition" (two hundred acres were deeded back to him as part of the settlement), where he had a large vineyard mostly west of Verdugo Road as it drives south over the pass into Eagle Rock. At the time, the area of the pass was called the Portozuelo, as was his ranch (also a similarly named pass at the western end of the Rancho La Canada, at what is now Foothill Boulevard between Lowell and Tujunga Canyon Boulevards). His house has not survived, but it was in the vicinity of the east side of Verdugo, near the corner of Acacia; news articles provide some proof of this. Some extant descriptions and drawings of the house suggest that it was not much

# Appendix 1

different than the Catalina Verdugo adobe: one story, with a veranda in front. Perhaps this is the prototype of the Verdugos' collection of casitas, as it was the typical form of almost all other California rancho buildings in their original construction, before later remodeling added second stories.

As a poignant reminder of the vineyard history in Glendale, there is this story: in a photo of a 1925 housing development called "Acacia Hills" near the intersection of Verdugo and Acacia, one can see the remnant of Julio's vineyard still on the hillside as the new houses are being built.

This seems to be the current explanation until further research uncovers new evidence or new surmises.

*The author wishes to thank George Ellison, retired special collections librarian of Glendale Public Library; Bill A'Hearn, at Glendale Public Works; Jay Platt, historical planner for the City of Glendale; and Katherine Yamada, Verdugo Views columnist for* Glendale News Press *for their invaluable suggestions and contributions.*

*Appendix 2*

# MAP OF THE RANCHO SAN RAPHAEL ("LA ZANJA") AND PRESENT-DAY GLENDALE

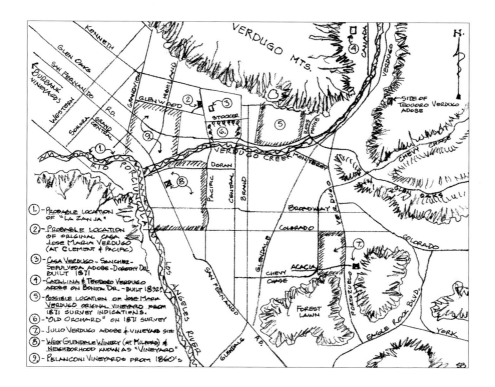

*Appendix 3*

# THE GRAPES AND WINE OF LOS ANGELES

## By Mathew Keller

Annual Report of the Commissioner of Patents
United States Patent Office,
February 25, 1859

The county of Los Angeles has one million five hundred and ten thousand bearing vines, and eight hundred and seventy-five thousand which were not productive last year, while preparations are being made to plant a million cuttings this season. Our climate and soil appear to be congenial to the growth.

For several years we have shipped to San Francisco large amounts of grapes, but since the vineyards of the northern part of the State have begun to bear, the trade has diminished, although ours are superior. The advantage, however, of the northern fruit is, that it can be brought fresh to market every morning. Consequently, we must more generally convert our grapes into wine. According to the books of the great forwarding house of P. Banning, at San Pedro, the amount shipped to San Francisco, in 1857, was 21,000 boxes, averaging 45 pounds each, and 250,000 gallons of wine; in 1858, 19,000 boxes, averaging 42 pounds each, and 325,000 gallons; the wine having been manufactured in the years mentioned, and principally by three houses, as many of the owners of vineyards have neither the means nor knowledge requisite for this purpose. Of the quantity indicated,

# Appendix 3

    Sainsevaine Brothers made..........................120,000 gallons
    Kohler & Frohling........................................80,000 "
    Mr. Keller..................................................50,000 "
    Scattering...................................................75,000 "

    Although this amount may seem large, yet not more than half our grapes are thus manufactured. The natives dry and lose much of the fruit, for want of proper fences; a considerable portion is shipped in various directions, and the Indian consumption is extensive. A vine yard, well grown and kept, will yield an average of a gallon of strong wine to the vine, and some vineyards average 2 gallons. I have a vineyard fifty-five years old, which, although badly managed in former times, averages $2\frac{1}{4}$ gallons to a vine.

    It is stated that the grape in cultivation is a variety introduced by the early Mission priests from San Carlos, in Catalonia, Spain, and first propagated from seed, which evidently had the effect of changing its quality, as well as adapting it to the climate and soil—yet other accounts assign it a different origin. Since then the invariable mode of propagation has been by cuttings, under the rudest and most careless culture, consisting of merely scratching over the surface with a wooden plough, sometimes laying off the ground in squares, with a distance of 2 varas [Spanish yards] between the vines, each way, or planting without line or row, making a hole $2\frac{1}{2}$ feet down with a crow-bar. Yet, under such treatment, the memory of the oldest inhabitant does not recall a season in which the grape crop of Los Angeles was not abundant. No manure has ever been used, nor should any of a vegetable character be employed, when the object is to make good wine, except leaves and other parts of the vine itself, cut, dried, and returned to the soil.

    Although Americans are now planting vineyards extensively, they follow the old system, only ploughing, and laying off better, not choosing to make innovations upon a mode that has been and is so successful. Doubtless, the manner of planting from nurseries, as practiced by the most intelligent vine-culturists of Europe, would be more economical and certain, where the vines remain two years in the nursery, and are transplanted in the third. The advantages would be, first, the use of the ground intended for the vineyard; secondly, the plants could be selected, so as to be all vigorous, and admitting of no failures, as in the case of cuttings; thirdly, in transplanting them, they could be set erect, thus rendering staking unnecessary—an item of great saving; fourth, the holes being larger, the roots would be better accommodated, and the loose soil, also, would constitute a great improvement on the crow-bar system; fifth, saving of labor in cultivating an extensive are of group for two

## Appendix 3

years; sixth, young vines would not be allowed to bear in the third year, as desired by the old mode, but being transplanted at the period, would form a new series of roots, become more vigorous, and produce a larger crop in the fourth year. Bearing a crop the third year certainly debilitates them.

Los Angeles is situated in latitude 34° north, which is within the favored region natural to the vine, and accounts for the abundance and certainty of our crops, while the little labor we expend in its culture insures our profit. Had it been otherwise, with high rate of California wages, failure would be inevitable. Planting a new vineyard, with us, costs about $10 or $12 an acre. Similar work in Ohio, with the terracing and trellising necessary there, costs from $400 to $500. Our vines are placed 6 feet apart, each way, in squares, leaving lanes and margins. This gives 1,100 to the acre, when well grown, 1,100 gallons of wine. In Ohio, 2,420 vines to an acre produce on an average of from eight to ten years, 250 gallons. The best vineyards of Bordeaux furnish 126 gallons to an acre of nearly 3,000 vines. Thus it is evident that this section is adapted to the vine and to the manufacture of genuine wine, without factitious aids. We need capital to develop our capabilities. As yet, there has been no fair test of our wines, as we are in the beginning, and cannot afford to wait until they have age. We expose them for sale, regardless of reputation, a few months after they are made, and are satisfied that they find purchasers. But we are convinced that if California wines had the same age as many of foreign production, which command exorbitant prices, ours would far surpass them. The sparkling wine made by Sainsevaine Brothers, of this place, has been well received everywhere, although comparatively new.

The wild grape abounds in all parts of this county, and there appear to be three varieties—one a rambling kind, producing little or no fruit; another less rambling, but still raising itself from the ground some distance, and furnishing heavy crops of well shaped bunches, fruit large and thin-skinned, and juice saccharine with well developed vinous flavor; and a third, which climbs to the top of the tallest trees, bearing light bunches of small fruits. Old Californians assure me that they formerly made excellent wine from this second variety, resembling in flavor, color, and aroma, the clarets of Bordeaux. It is replete with coloring matter, and I have no doubt that, if properly tested, it will prove an invaluable acquisition to the State. Our cultivated grape has not equally good qualities for making wines of the red as of the white class; it is deficient in color.

It is also said that this variety of the wild grape produced better aguadiente (brandy) that the cultivated fruit, which, in Lower California, among the ruins of the Missions, is white and red, of the Malaga type, introduced by the Jesuits by way of Peru, and is part of superior quality both for wine and for the table. The greater part, however, is converted into raisins.

Various foreign grapes have been tried here, but none succeed so well as that now in cultivation. The famous Catawba and Isabella have been experimented with for several years, and at last thrown into the road as useless. If we ever obtain a better variety, it must be from seeds. The great vineyards which were attached to the Missions of California, with few exceptions, are ruined and dead. That of San Gabriel, in this county, had two hundred thousand vines, of which remain but black stumps to mark the ruin. Let us have a railroad, and we will supply the Union with grapes and wine.

Most of our vineyard labor is done by the Indians, some of whom are the best pruners we have—an art they learned from the Mission Fathers.

# Manufacture of Wine

The manufacture of wine, in a suitable climate, is simple, and may be done by any one of ordinary intelligence. But when the climate and soil are not adapted to the nature of the grape, then, indeed, it becomes a complicated art. One of the most essential things to be observed in its manufacture is the proper regulation of temperature, particularly during the phenomenon of the first fermentation; and to this the least attention is paid. If the must is too cool, the fermentation is slow and apt to sour, while, if there is too much heat, it will soon go into the acetous state. Must, which abounds in saccharine matter, and is deficient in ferment, requires a higher degree of temperature than that which has these substances in opposite proportions. The strongest must, even when it contains much ferment, can support a higher temperature than the weak, because the great quantity of alcohol which is developed, retards the action of the ferment, and prevents the tendency to pass to the acetous fermentation. The best general temperature is between 62° and 64° F. There is little difficulty in maintaining this temperature in a cellar, but it may be observed that the act of fermentation elevates the temperature. To arrive at that which is the most convenient, it is necessary to pay attention to the temperature of the grapes at the time of mashing them. If picked early in the morning, or at noon, it varies many degrees. To obviate this, they may be picked a day in advance, or they should be cooled in a large vat, and *vice versa*. The temperature of substances cast to the surface during fermentation

# Appendix 3

is more elevated than the liquid which supports them, and if their contact with the air is prolonged, they experience alterations of another nature.

These few facts comprehend all that is necessary to make wine, but they are subject to many variations and much detail, like most other processes of manufacture.

The manner of making wine, in this county, is as follows: The grapes are deprived of their stems by hand; they are then mashed between wooden or iron rollers; some tread them out in the ancient style. A portion of the juice runs into a cooling vat, without pressing; the crushed grapes are put into a screw-press and forced out rapidly, all the result being must for white wine. As the grapes are black, and the coloring matter exists only in the skin, and requires in some degree the presence of alcohol to dissolve it, if the pressing be done quickly, the wine will be white; but if slowly, or if the grapes come broken from the vineyard, the must will show color; for, as soon as the fruit is broken, and the juice comes in contact with the air, fermentation commences, and simultaneous with it, the prescence of alcohol, in a greater or less degree, which extracts the coloring matter. The must is then transferred into the fermenting tuns, and the first active fermentation goes on, according to circumstances, for from four to ten days. The mashed grapes are put into vats to ferment, from which results red wine. This is, in part, distilled into brandy. Some persons distil red wine with the "marc" into brandy immediately after fermentation, but if left to pass a secondary fermentation, it would yield more alcohol.

The wine is racked off in January and February, again in March and April, and for the third time in September. It should be taken off the lees after the first fermentation subsides, when the wine has settled; for it cannot gain anything by being allowed to stand on the lees longer than is absolutely necessary.

The proportions of saccharine matter and ferment in our grapes are well balanced; therefore there is no extraordinary art in making wine; as it will make itself, with common care and without the addition of any extraneous substance. The purest and finest wines in the world are made from the juice of the grape alone.

More capital is needed to make property cellars, procure necessary materials, and to enable us to hold our wines till they have age, when they would compare favorable with the best. Another great want is a bottle manufactory, that we may store our wines, and prevent counterfeiting, which is now going on extensively.

A poor woman in the adjoining county of Santa Barbara has but one vine. It bore last year five thousand bunches of beautiful grapes weighing

# Appendix 3

over a pound each, yielding her the handsome sum of $400. When a girl, and leaving Monterey to remove to her present home, she picked up a vine cutting to drive her mule. This cutting she planted upon her arrival, and, after the lapse of seventy years, such is the result.

*Appendix 4*

# MATHEW KELLER OBITUARY

## An Old Landmark Gone
## *Los Angeles Herald*, April 12, 1881

The people of Los Angeles were much shocked yesterday by intelligence of the death of Matthew I. Keller, familiarly known as Don Mateo Keller, which took place at his late residence on Alameda street at nine o'clock yesterday morning. The event was not expected, although Mr. Keller had been ailing for some weeks. After having been confined to his bed for quite a spell he rallied and was strong enough to be driven out. It was a matter of general remark amongst the friends who saw him on these occasions that his constitution was irreparably broken, but few of them expected to hear of his death so soon. While eating his breakfaster yesterday morning, Mrs. Stuhr, wife of the Superintendent of his winery, had occasion to leave the room to procure some necessary article and, though absent but for a moment, on her return she found him dead in his chair. Dr. Wise pronounced heart disease the immediate cause of his death. We take the following resume of Mr. Keller's career from the *Express* of yesterday evening: Mr. Keller was born in Cork, Ireland, in 1811. He emigrated to this county soon after attaining his majority. Little is known of his early career, except that he was in Mexico during the war, accompanying the American army as a trader. He was naturalized in New Orleans in 1849. He settled in Los Angeles about the year 1850, and began as a merchant, having a store on the southwest corner of Commercial and Los Angeles streets. He devoted himself to this business

# Appendix 4

six or seven years, later finding a remunerative trade in packing and shipping grapes. From dealing in grapes he soon drifted into raising them, when he gave up merchandizing altogether. For more than twenty years he has been known as one of the prominent and extensive wine producers in the county. Recently younger and more active men have surpassed in the quantity of wine and brandy which they have made, but none have turned out a better quality. Five years ago Mr. Keller found himself in somewhat straightened circumstances by reason of the stringency of the times generally and the especial depress of the wine industry. He had a large quantity of wine on hand for which there was no market, and, at the same time, heavy debts at a high rate of interest were pressing upon him. Under the pressure of these circumstances he took up his residence in New York City, where he remained for about a year, devoting his personal attention to opening a market for his products. His efforts were remarkably successful, as he sold every spare gallon of his wines, and, with the proceeds, it is gratifying to say, he had enough to discharge his obligations, and placed himself in easy financial circumstances. Within the past year he had been planting new vineyards and making arrangements to increase his business by a marked degree. The estate which he leaves is a valuable one, embracing the home place on Alameda street—about twenty acres—and the Rising Sun Vineyard, in the southern suburbs, of 150 acres, the Vines being from twenty to twenty five years old. The wine and brandy manufactory and cellars are located on the home place, Alameda Street. The machinery has a capacity for crushing fifty tons of grapes in a day, and turns out, during the season, 200 gallons of brandy and 1,000 gallons of wine daily. The estate also includes the Malaga ranch, on the coast above Santa Monica, running out to Point Dumas. Mr. Keller planted five hundred acres of vineyard on this ranch during the past two seasons. Mr. Keller's preference was Malvosie and Mission vines for heavy wines, and he often said that there was no better than the ordinary Mission for all the purposes of a vigueron. He thought the Blaue Elbe had not good keeping qualities. His manufactures of wines were Madeiras, Sherries and Port, and upon these he established quite a reputation; especially the sherry, taking diplomas at our local Fairs and carrying off a silver medal from the Centennial at Philadelphia. The wine cellars, of which there are two, one 60x60 and the other 50x300—are located on the home place adjoining the works. With all the old stock sold and only the vintage of 1879 on hand, he still had one hundred thousand gallons of wine in store. Mr. Keller was the first man to raise cotton in California, receiving a premium of $1,000 or upward from the State therefor. The cotton was produced during the

# Appendix 4

early years of the war of the Rebellion. Deceased was a man notable for his physical and intellectual vigor. His robust frame and blonde hair, in which scarcely a streak of gray could be detected, gave him the appearance of a man of not over fifty years of age. His friends were frequently in the habit of rallying him on his healthy and youthful appearance, and most of them thought the old gentleman, although past seventy, was good for ten years of life. Universally known in Southern California and a favorite with great numbers of our people, the death of this useful citizen and worthy man will cast a pall over a large circle.

*Appendix 5*

# INTERVIEW WITH GEORGES LE MESNAGER

## Los Angeles Wines
### Angeleno Vigneron Thinks They Are Good
### *Los Angeles Herald*, June 6, 1889

Yesterday, a *Herald* reporter held a conversation of half an hour with Geo. L. Mesnager, a well-known vine-grower of this city. In the course of the talk Mr. Mesnager said:

We are making satisfactory progress with the business of making wines. We still have a good deal to learn. So have the consumers of wine.

Yes, we make an excellent port wine. It is as good as any made in any part of Europe. Now you see there are only certain districts in Europe where, after centuries of experience, they try to make port. It has been learned that this sort of wine is good made from the grapes of certain localities and poor outside of them. They no longer try to make it where it has been found not to be good.

No, we do not make good sherry. Ah! You see there is only one little spot in all Europe where they make really good sherry. For so many years the wine-makers have tried to make sherry, but it is good only in one small district. Maybe we shall discover by and by the sherry district of California. It may be in Los Angeles county, or in some other part of Southern California, Los Angeles county is as large as a good slice of Europe. Many things may be found here in time. We have found that Los Angeles and San Bernardino grapes make the best ports; in fact they are the only port districts in the State.

# Appendix 5

Of course there is a good deal in the way grapes are handled. It will not pay to take the pains they take in Europe. We might discover a bit of land where wines like those of the Chateau Lafitte might grow. But remember in all France there is only one Chateau Lafitte. In all Europe there is only one Chateau Lafitte. We have to study these things, and then in time, we shall know what sort of wines grapes from certain localities will make. I will take as much trouble in the making of my wines as they do in France, as they do at the Chateau Lafitte, when the market will warrant it. At present it will not. I have in my cellar wines as good as the best make in Roussillon, France. Connoisseurs who know perfectly the qualities of the wines of Roussillon have tasted the wine and they say they are as good as they ever found in France. They are four years old, and are perfect. In France they would sell for $2 a gallon. Here I cannot sell them. I know that at hotels and restaurants some people pay $1 a bottle, or at the rate of $5 or $6 a gallon, for good clarets; but they are not many, and those who do, want a French wine, or rather a French label, for very often the wine is of native growth, with a foreign label on the bottle. The consumers are deceived, but not cheated. They get as good or better wine, but they are humbugged in the label. When I can get $2 a gallon for perfect wines, I will hand-pick each grape. Lafitte sells in France at $2 a bottle, and labor is cheap there. So is money. It costs something in interest for us to carry vintage four years.

Yes, we can make good light table wines. I am telling you of an excellent wine. It carries no more alcohol than it should do. But we must not think we can make good port, good Burgundies, good Rhine wines and good sherry all on the same patch of land. Our vineyards where we make our clarets are high up the sides of the mountains, they are covered with snow every winter. They are 2,500 feet or more above the sea level. They are steep slopes where it is hard to plow.

So you see we are learning. In time we shall make other sorts of wine as successfully as we are making ports, as successfully as I am making my Roussillon red wines. But the consumers will also have to learn to buy wines on their merits and not on their labels. They will also have to learn that there are different grades, and that they will have to pay more for wines carefully made, intelligently treated and kept until they mature, than they pay for the stuff called wine which is so often made without care, and sold as soon as the first fermentation is over.

*Appendix 6*

# RAMBAUD'S ROW

## Threatens the Life of His Landlord and Is Put Under Bonds

### Los Angeles Herald, August 31, 1898

For an hour or two yesterday Justice Young's court resembled the Latin Quarter of Paris during a student's row. Frenchmen were jabbering away at one another and at the court, swinging their arms and generally settling a case at bar among themselves. The cause on trial was a charge brought by G.L. Mesnager against Emile Rambaud for threatening his life.

Rambaud rents a vineyard owned by Mesnager's wife, the husband being her agent. A day or two ago Mesnager drove a couple of friends out to the vineyard and through it. Rambaud objected to the presence of visitors uninvited by himself, objected with rocks, sticks, stones, etc., accompanied with volleys of choice French expletives.

But it was not until Rambaud tied up Mesnager's buggy to a tree with a rope and threatened to shoot the man that untied it that Mesnager really believed his life was in danger. The trial was only interesting because the court could not understand what the witnesses were saying and every once in awhile the witness would make a statement in French which, before it could be interpreted, the Frenchmen in the courtroom would approve or object to and "there you are."

"They waved arms, shook fists and said things until Justice Young, through the interpreter, made it clear to them that any further demonstration would land them in jail."

# Appendix 6

The end of the case was that the irascible Rambaud was bound over in the sum of $500. To keep the peace, he gave bonds and was released from the custody of the constable.

# BIBLIOGRAPHY

To avoid repetition, a source is cited only when it occurs first, regardless of use in later chapters.

## INTRODUCTION

Pinney, Thomas. *History of Wine in America.* Vol. 1, *From the Beginnings to Prohibition.* Berkeley: University of California Press, 1989.
———. *History of Wine in America.* Vol. 2, *From Prohibition to the Present.* Berkeley: University of California Press, first paperback printing 2007.

These volumes are a tremendous achievement in wine scholarship (or any scholarship, for that matter), exhausting in detail, wide-ranging in scope. There is nothing quite like them. They are the primary resources for this work.

## CHAPTER 1: THE SPANISH MISSION'S

Amerine, M.A., and V.L. Singleton. *Wine: An Introduction for Americans.* Berkeley: University of California Press, 1975.
Brady, Roy. "Alta California's First Vintage." In *University of California/Sotheby's Book of Wine,* edited by Doris Muscatine, Maynard Amerine and Bob Thompson, 10–15. Berkeley: University of California Press/Sotheby Public, 1984.

# Bibliography

Crow, John A. *Spain: The Root and the Flower.* Berkeley: University of California Press, 1985.

Leggett, Herbert B. *Early History of Wine Production in California.* Wine Institute, San Francisco, April 2, 1941 (a private publication of the Wine Institute).

Muscatine, Doris, Maynard Amerine and Bob Thompson, eds. *University of California/Sotheby's Book of California Wine.* Berkeley: University of California Press/Sotheby Public, 1984.

Rolle, Andrew F. *California: A History.* 3rd edition. Wheeling, IL: Harlan, Davidson, Inc., 1978.

Weber, Monsignor Francis J., editor. *San Gabriel, San Fernando, San Luis Rey, San Jose,* et al. Los Angeles: Archdiocese of Los Angeles, n.d. (Each mission book is a subject of relevant documentation on its history.)

Winepros.org.

## Chapter 2: Early Winemakers and Vineyards

Cleland, Robert Glass. *The Cattle on a Thousand Hills.* San Marino, CA: Huntington Library and Art Gallery, 5th printing, 1990.

Engstrand, Iris. "Early California Viniculture: 1830–1865." *Southern California Historical Anthology*, a centennial publication of 1984.

Graham, Otis, Jr., et al. *Aged in Oak: The Story of the Santa Barbara County Wine Industry.* Santa Barbara: University of California, South Coast Historical Series, 1998.

Robinson, W.W. *Land in California.* Berkeley: University of California Press, 1979 edition.

## Chapter 3: Jean Louis Vignes, William Wolfskill and the Sainsevains

Carosso, Vincent P. *The California Wine Industry: 1830–1895.* Berkeley: University of California Press, 1951.

Davis, William Heath. *Seventy-five Years in California.* San Francisco: J. Howell, 1929.

Gumprecht, Blake. *The Los Angeles River.* Baltimore, MD: Johns Hopkins University Press, 2001.

Vignes family papers. Seaver Center for Western History, Natural History Museum, County of Los Angeles.

Bibliography

# Chapter 4: The Gold Rush and After

Creason, Glen. *Los Angeles in Maps.* New York: Rizzoli, 2010.
Newmark, Harris. *Sixty Years in California: 1853–1913.* Edited by Maurice and Marco Newmark. Los Angeles: Zeitlin+ Ver Brugge, 4th edition, 1970.
Pitt, Leonard. *Decline of the Californios: A Social History of the Spanish-Speaking Californias, 1846–1890.* Berkeley: University of California Press, 1966.
Read, Nat. B. *Don Benito Wilson: Mountain Man to Mayor, Los Angeles 1841–1878.* Los Angeles: Angel City Press, 2008.

# Chapter 5: Developments in the Valleys

Dinkelspiel, Frances. *Towers of Gold.* New York: St. Martin's Press, 2008.
Nadeau, Remi. *City Makers: The Story of Southern California's First Boom, 1869–1876.* Los Angeles: Trans-Anglo Books, 1965.
Rose, L.J., Jr. *L.J. Rose of Sunny Slope: 1827–1899.* San Marino, CA: Huntington Library, 1959.

# Chapter 6: Anaheim

MacArthur, Mildred Yorba. *Anaheim, the Mother Colony.* Los Angeles: Ward Ritchie Press, 1959.

# Chapter 7: Rise of the North

*California Wine.* Palo Alto, CA: Lane Magazine and Book Company, 1973.
Johnson, Hugh. *Story of Wine.* London: Mitchell Beazley, 1999.

# Chapter 8: Decline in the South

Lothrop, Gloria Ricci. "The Boom of the '80's Revisited." *Land Policy and Land Use in Southern California.* Historical Society of Southern California, Fall/Winter 1993.

Masters, Nathan. "El Aliso: Ancient Sycamore Was Silent Witness to Four Centuries of Los Angeles History." *SoCal Focus*, KCET.org, June 27, 2012.
Newcombe, John. *Rancho La Canada*. DVD, 2007.
Robinson, W.W. *Panoramas: A Picture History of Southern California*. Los Angeles: Title Insurance and Trust Co., 1953.

## Chapter 9: Turn of the Century through Prohibition

Brown, John, Jr., and James Boyd, eds. *San Bernardino and Riverside History, Vol. III*. Riverside, CA: Lewis Publishing Co., 1922.
Burns, Ken. *Prohibition* (DVD), 2012.
City of Burbank. *Burbank, a Centennial History*. Burbank, CA: self-published, 2011.
El Pueblo de Los Angeles.org.
Hathaway & Associates. *Historic and Architectural Historic Survey for the Le Mesnager Vineyard Ranch*. Crestline, CA: self-published, 1991.
*Italian Vineyard Co*. Souvenir booklet from the winery, 1915. Cal Poly Pomona Library: Special Collections.
*Los Angeles Herald*. "Southern California Wine Industry." September 3, 1905.
Newcombe, Robert. *Images of America: Montrose*. Charleston, SC: Arcadia Publishing, 2013.
Oberbeck, Grace J. *A History of La Crescenta and La Canada Valleys*. La Crescenta, CA: *Crescenta Valley Ledger*, 1938.
Perry, E. Caswell. *Burbank: An Illustrated History*. Burbank, CA: Windsor Publications, 1987.
Sadler, Jo Anne. *Crescenta Valley Pioneers and Their Legacies*. Charleston, SC: The History Press, 2012.
Yamada, Katherine. "Neighborhood [Pelanconi] Steeped in History," Verdugo Views, *Glendale News-Press*, April 25, 2008.

## Chapter 10: From Repeal to the Present

Biane, Philo (Oral History). *Wine Making in Southern California & Recollections of Fruit Industries, Ltd*. Interview by Ruth Teiser, photos by Katherine Harroun, introduction by Maynard Amerine. August 1–14, 1969. Berkeley: Regents of University of California, 1972. (A long, detailed and

# Bibliography

fascinating discussion of all phases of vineyard growing and winemaking, cellaring and selling, by a man and generations of his family who have been doing it all. It is essentially Winemaking 101.)

Cal Poly Pomona Library Special Collections. Oral Histories of Cucamonga Valley Winemakers.

City of Rancho Cucamonga. Oral Histories of Valley Winemakers.

Ginoffwine: Winegrowing, Winemaking and More. Ginoffvine.wordpress.com.

*Author's Note*: In the early 1960s, my family would spend months of the summer on a lemon orchard ranch in Alta Loma (now part of Rancho Cucamonga), near the corner of Haven Avenue and Highland. My father was an architect, whose client was the orchard's owners, Stan and Ruth Allen. They would go on extended vacations, and during that time, we would take care of the ranch, as construction on the house was taking place. Being little boys, my brothers and I would play in the lemon grove and in the vineyard next door to the west, the Opici Winery. Often we would sneak into the winery building, savoring its cool, dark depths as shelter from the summer sun, and just stand there, breathing in the intoxicating aroma of fermenting wine. The winery workers were benevolent to our trespassing, one going so far as to show us the vats of percolating grapes (it could have been Hubert Opici himself, educating future wine drinkers). Driving around the valley, we'd pass along the roads marked by fieldstone gutters and embankments, shaded by miles of towering eucalyptus trees, dividing acre after acre of vineyards and citrus groves extending seemingly to the horizon. We were too young to know just how iconic this landscape is (was) to Southern California. This agricultural trinity—citrus, grapevines and eucalyptus—has come to define part of the vision of California, a vision that is slowly passing into history as the pastoral life is swept away by massive, heedless urbanization and a vision celebrated in art and literature as a dream of ease and beauty and the good life under a beneficent sun in a cloudless, blue sky. It is a vision that will be lost or denigrated, unless it is firmly fixed in the memory and imagination of each passing generation. This "trinity" is like most Californians: they all came from somewhere else and found the soil here perfect to put down roots and thrive. Most of the rural landscape is gone now. The Opici Winery and vineyard has become (appropriately) Vineyard Junior High School. The lemon groves and giant eucalyptus trees have been pulled out for housing tracts and road widening. Yet the little houses that my father and the Allens built so long ago are still there, fanning out from the main house in their own grove of towering eucalyptus.

# INDEX

**A**

Alhambra  54, 86
Anaheim  71, 87, 89
Angelica wine  21, 45, 57

**B**

Baldwin, E.J. "Lucky"  58, 61, 110
Boyle, Andrew  27, 35, 43
Brookside Winery  46, 82, 100, 115
Brusso family  95
Brusso Winery  110
Burbank, David  63

**C**

Chapman, Joseph  26, 57
Childs, Ozro W.  59
Crescenta Valley  110
Cucamonga  12, 28, 40, 66, 87, 114

**D**

Downey, Governor John  64, 77
Dreyfus, Benjamin  53, 73, 85

**E**

El Aliso  11, 34

**F**

Frohling, John  44, 71

**G**

Galleano Winery  114, 115
Guasti, Secundo  70, 97

**H**

Haraszthy, Agoston  76
Hellman, Isaias W.  44, 64, 79

**J**

Jesuit  15, 134

**K**

Keller, Mathew "Don Mateo"  12, 29, 42, 46, 64, 131, 137
Kohler, Charles  13, 44, 71

# Index

## L

La Zanja  24, 121
Le Mesnager, Georges  82, 141, 143
Le Mesnager, Louis  92
Los Angeles River  11, 24, 47, 99, 123

## M

Mission Winery  100

## N

Nadeau, Remi  81
Newmark, Harris  42, 60

## P

Pasadena  51, 54, 110
Patton, George Smith  66, 88
Pelanconi, Antonio  27, 47
Pelanconi vineyards  109
Pelanconi Winery  97
phylloxera  58, 66

## R

Rancho San Rafael  24
Rancho Topanga-Malibu-Sequit  29, 43

## S

Sainsevain brothers  13, 33, 37, 43, 45, 83, 90, 132
Sainsevain, Jean Louis  35, 37, 64
Sainsevain, Pierre  34, 37
San Gabriel  49
San Gabriel mission  22
San Juan Capistrano  17
Santa Anita  59
Scott, Jonathan  59
Serra, Junipero  15, 58
Shorb, James De Barth  52, 66, 85
Sonoma  19, 69, 75

## T

Tapia, Tiburcio  28, 63, 66, 119

## V

Vache Freres  46, 82, 115
Verdugo, Catalina  62, 124
Verdugo, Jose Maria  23, 47, 121
Verdugo, Julio  62, 125
Vignes, Jean Louis  11, 26, 33, 37, 46, 90, 95
Virginia Dare Winery  104, 118

## W

West Glendale Winery  93, 99, 109, 124
Wilson, Benjamin D. "Don Benito"  13, 29, 49
Wolfskill, William  26, 33, 36, 60, 72
Workman, William H.  28

## Z

Zalvidea, Jose  19

# ABOUT THE AUTHOR

Stuart Douglass Byles is a native Angeleno, raised in Pasadena. He attended Pasadena City College and Reed College in Portland, Oregon, as a history major. He makes his living as a designer/builder of residences, primarily in historical styles. He has been a longtime docent at the Gamble House museum in Pasadena. He is a founding member of the Historical Society of the Crescenta Valley and its current vice-president. He is a founding member of the Stone Barn Vineyard Conservancy, a sponsored volunteer organization of the historical society, set up in 2007 to promote and celebrate the wine history of the surrounding area and maintain the commemorative vineyard at the Deukmejian Wilderness Park in Glendale.

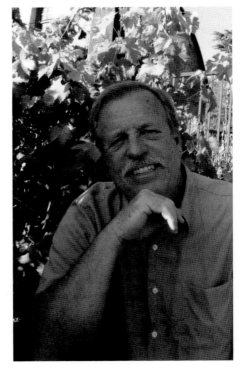

*Visit us at*
www.historypress.net

This title is also available as an e-book